What Others Are Saying About Chris DuPré and *The Wild Love of God...*

Wow! What a book. What a story. *The Wild Love of God* is a journey of radical forgiveness. In it, Chris DuPré gives us his life message: the unconditional, healing, transforming love of our heavenly Father. Chris's personal transformation brought healing and life into the painful memories of his upbringing with his father, a former WWII POW. Reading this book is like watching a beautiful miracle unfold as deep healing takes place first in the son and then in the heart of his father, who needs forgiveness to have his own freedom. I laughed and I wept as I read this wonderful gift to us all.

—*Bill Johnson*
Senior pastor, Bethel Church, Redding, California
Author, *When Heaven Invades Earth* and *Defining Moments*

In his book, *The Wild Love of God*, Chris DuPré touches the hearts of us all. He tells a story of pain that everyone can relate to and shows how forgiveness and the Father's love bring life and peace. *The Wild Love of God* is a joyous read and a life-changing message!

—*John Arnott*
Founding pastor, Catch the Fire Ministries
(Formally Toronto Airport Christian Fellowship)

Like a voice crying out in the wilderness, my friend Chris DuPré brings us a treasure that releases echoes of the Father's relentless heartbeat right into the very essence of who you are. Do you want to know the amazing love of God? Would you like to encounter His persistent presence? Do you need healing from a father-heart wound? Then this book was written with you in mind. Chris's life message is contained in *The Wild Love of God*. The only thing it lacks is a warning label: "The contents of this book could change your life!" I highly commend to you this inspiring book, *The Wild Love of God*!

—*James Goll*
Encounters Network, Prayer Storm, Compassion Acts
Author, *The Seer, The Lost Art of Intercession*, and
Passionate Pursuit

It is with great joy that I recommend Chris DuPré's new book, *The Wild Love of God*. You are not just about to read a story of God's affection; you are about to find yourself in the middle of His gaze of love for you. As a longtime friend of Chris's, I know that he writes about what he knows. As you read his story, you, too, will begin to see the depth of God's heart for you. When you know His heart, it changes everything!

—*Mike Bickle*
Founder and director, International House of Prayer,
Kansas City, Missouri

The Wild Love of God by Chris DuPré is not your ordinary, run-of-the-mill Christian book. Rather, it is an eloquent and penetrating glimpse into the heart of a man who has found the depths of God's love in the midst of profound hardship. I encourage you to read and ponder the life of my friend and his journey to become a friend of God. Chris's incredible story will pull you away from the sidelines of mediocrity onto the playing field of extraordinary adventures in God.

—*Larry Randolph*
Author, *User-Friendly Prophecy* and *Original Breath*

CHRIS DUPRÉ

FOREWORD BY MIKE BICKLE

THE WILD LOVE OF GOD

A JOURNEY THAT HEALS LIFE'S DEEPEST WOUNDS

WHITAKER HOUSE

THE WILD LOVE OF GOD:
A Journey That Heals Life's Deepest Wounds

www.chrisdupre.com
chrisdopray@comcast.net

ISBN: 978-1-62911-674-7
eBook ISBN 978-1-62911-675-4
Printed in the United States of America
© 2016 by Chris DuPré

Whitaker House
1030 Hunt Valley Circle
New Kensington, PA 15068
www.whitakerhouse.com

Library of Congress Cataloging-in-Publication Data

Names: DuPré, Chris, 1954- author.
Title: The wild love of God : journey into the love that heals life's deepest wounds / by Chris DuPré.
Description: New Kensington, PA : Whitaker House, 2016.
Identifiers: LCCN 2016001672 | ISBN 9781629116747 (trade pbk. : alk. paper)
Subjects: LCSH: DuPré, Chris, 1954- | DuPré, David J., -1991. | Fathers and sons—Religious aspects—Christianity. | Forgiveness--Religious aspects—Christianity. | Christian biography.
Classification: LCC BR1725.D74 A3 2016 | DDC 277.3/082092—dc23
LC record available at http://lccn.loc.gov/2016001672

1 2 3 4 5 6 7 8 9 10 11 ⨎ 23 22 21 20 19 18 17 16

DEDICATION

I want to dedicate this book to my father and mother, David J. DuPré and Mary Kay DuPré. From two very different perspectives, you both showed me how deeply God loves. Dad, a man of deep emotions: you showed me the depths of His affection. Mom, a woman of valor and my hero: you unveiled to me over the years the steadfast love of the Lord. My love for both of you will never end.

CONTENTS

FOREWORD

A heart ravished by the love of God becomes a force, both to love God and to love others. I've known Chris DuPré for over twenty years, and he is a man whose heart has been overwhelmed by the love of God. His understanding of the Father's heart has touched and transformed countless lives, mine included.

I first met Chris in the early 1990s, when he and his precious family moved to Kansas City. As our new seventh-grade teacher, he became the first person outside the home to teach my youngest son. That initial place of common ground brought us together as teachers and fathers, and then as friends.

Chris is a master storyteller. For decades, he has unveiled God's love through his anointed music, his teachings, and his life. Now, after hearing encouragement from me for years to do this, he has finally recorded his story and his revelation of God's great affection. What Chris has written will forever change the way you look into the eyes of God and understand how He sees you.

What makes his writing effective is the fact that Chris does not just write about God's heart; he also lives as one who releases the heart of God on a daily basis. I have not only looked into his eyes and found love there, but I have witnessed, time and again, other individuals who, not knowing Chris, have approached him tentatively, only to be enveloped by the Father's love coming through his smile, his kind eyes, and his warm embrace. Chris DuPré is the real thing.

The book you are about to read is the result of more than mere hours of work in front of a desk—it's the fruit of a lifetime of gathering. Chris has immersed himself in the Father's love so that others may know and experience that same great affection.

My heart is filled with joy over this book, and I am certain that it will take you deeper into the river of God's love, making you lovesick for an even closer dance with Him.

—*Mike Bickle*
Director, International House of Prayer Kansas City
Founder, International House of Prayer University
Author, *Growing in the Prophetic* and *Passion for Jesus*

ACKNOWLEDGMENTS

Paul Rogers: Thank you, Paul, for not only believing that I had something to say but also for helping me get it out. You are a true friend, and I thank God on a regular basis that you're in my life.

Renee DeLoriea: I could not have done this book without you. Your practical help and tireless patience with me have been such a blessing. Laura and I are big fans of yours!

Brad Cummings: My friend, you helped in more ways than I can say. Thank you for your generous heart and for helping me to see Him more clearly. I look forward to walking together with you for a long time.

Carol DuPré: I thank you with eternal gratitude for leading me into the arms of God. You helped bring a family who thought they knew Him into the reality of being His friend. Love you, Carol Babe.

Mark DuPré: Thank you for helping me sing. You gave me my voice. Even after all these years, I still need to know your thoughts on a matter. You're a wise man, and I'm honored to call you my brother and my best friend. I love you.

Mike Bickle: Thank you, my dear friend, for helping to add more theology and a greater understanding to what I had already known and experienced concerning the depth of God's love. You showed me the One who sees the "yes" in my heart, and it's changed my life forever. I love you.

Andrea, Katie, and Melissa: Being your father has been my joy and privilege. You've shown this dad how much it means to be loved by his children and, in so doing, have opened my eyes to understand how much my love means to God. Your imprint is all over this book. I love you three so much!

Laura DuPré: You are the love of my life, and I thank you for loving me back so well. We've had quite a journey so far, and your loving support has been there through it all. You are beautiful inside and out. Everyone who knows you knows how far I married up. You are my greatest gift from God. I love you, Laura DuPré!

INTRODUCTION

I wanted to write this book for a long time. Not because I wanted to get *my* book out there, but because I wanted to get the knowledge of *His heart* out there. During my thirty-seven-plus years of ministry, I've observed that all people, regardless of age, gender, and demographic, share at least one thing in common: they struggle with knowing—really knowing—that God sees them and loves them just for who they are, not for what they do.

I first met the Lord in 1973, and it felt as if I had happened upon a famous stranger in a dark alley and had been tasked with loving Him more and more, above anything else in my life. In the years since, I have heard the message "Love the Lord!" conveyed by preachers via teaching, yelling, weeping, joking, telling stories, telling even longer stories, and even ripping apart a phone book. Through a myriad of ways, I have been told to love Him more. The problem is, I have rarely been told *how* to love Him more.

Try loving someone more because you're told that you *need* to love that person more. It doesn't work. Try telling one of your kids to fall in love with the person you picked out instead of the person they've already fallen for. Two people might grow into love, over time, but telling people to "love more, right now!" just does not work. All it does is leave listeners with the idea that they are doing something wrong or that they have a deeper problem, such as a hard heart that, for some reason, just doesn't love to the degree that it should.

For those of us who love Jesus, it should be our joy not just to remind people to love Him with all of their hearts but to also give them a reason to fall more and more in love with Him. We need to unveil Him to the world. We need to reveal His heart. When we do that, others can't help but fall more in love with Him.

In fifth grade, I had a crush on a girl named Pat. I wrote her an elaborate letter that went something like this: "Do you like me?" I know—amazing, right? Below that, I drew two boxes: one marked "Yes," the other, "No." Between them, I wrote, "Check one." I was quite the romantic. I remember waiting for what seemed like an eternity for Pat's response. Turns out she liked me. I was jubilant. Why was her validation so important? Why was I waiting on pins and needles for her answer? Because we all live for the answer to the question, "Do you like me?"

The most important question anyone can ask is, "Is there a God?" But right on the heels of that question comes another,

"If there is a God, how does He feel about me?" Before we can decide how we feel about God, we need to know how He feels about us. That's the correct progression. And the answer to that question will determine how we live.

The apostle Paul exhorts us to come to the knowledge of the Son of God, so that we will *"no longer be children, tossed to and fro"* (Ephesians 4:13–14). The tendency of children is to follow. They are directed from the outside, as opposed to being moved from within. Mature believers, however, rooted and grounded in love, can embark on the journey to become greater lovers of God. But if we are unsure in our understanding of His heart, we will be forever trying to gain His favor instead of living out of the assurance of it.

Therefore, the question remains, "How does God see me?" When we discover the answer, we begin to walk out the rest of our lives.

I love how tender John the Apostle gets in his writings. He often addresses his readers as "little children" or just simply "beloved." These personal endearments help us get a handle on his heart, which God then uses to speak to us about His own heart.

One of the simplest and best-known Bible verses is also, if we see it right, one of the most empowering verses in the entire Book. It goes like this: *"We love Him because He first loved us"* (1 John 4:19). Very simple and, yes, very well-known. Yet it is the answer to the yearning in our hearts if we desire to love God more.

We love *because*. That *"because"* is everything. I could rephrase the verse like this: *"Because He loves us, we can love."* Or, "We have the capacity to love *because* He first fills us with the understanding of His love for us." Or even, "Our ability to love is directly related to our ability to know how deeply we are loved."

It reminds me of sixth-grade math class, where we first worked with bar graphs. If you were to label one bar "How much I know I am loved by God" and another one "How much I love," the second bar can only be as long as the first, never longer. My ability to love is always contingent upon my ability to see and understand God's love for me. I love *because*.

Why is that? Why do we have to know God's heart before we can fully love Him back? Ask a farmer to grow a seed without soil or water, and he'll look at you like you're crazy. Unless a seed has a place to take root, it will just sit there, full of potential that will never come to fruition. You can yell at it, tell it how big all the other seeds have grown, guilt it into growing, or teach it how it's supposed to grow; but, in the end, these efforts will prove fruitless—literally. Seeds are meant to be planted and rooted. And the same is true for us. We are meant to be planted in the truth of God's Word and to be rooted in the knowledge of His love. We can learn the language of love over time, and we can practice saying the right things, but correct words can never replace loved hearts.

During a recent speaking engagement at a church, I shared about the healing power of God's love, and then we had a time of questions and answers. After several attendees had thrown questions at me, I turned to one of the pastors and asked him a question: "What did the senior pastor preach on four weeks ago?" He stood there in silence for a moment, trying to recall the sermon from four weeks earlier, but he could not.

Finally, after a couple of minutes, someone in the crowd came up with the answer, and we all had a good laugh. I then asked the pastor if he could tell me, from beginning to end, the story of *The Wizard of Oz*. He chuckled, then proceeded to tell the story in great detail. It was a *story* that he could remember, not the words of a sermon.

Studies show that we retain only a fraction of what we hear. Most of what people take away from a message or a person is not the words but the impression made upon their minds and their hearts. Therefore, in order to share my heart "in words," I knew I had to do it through the story of my journey.

Not too long ago, I ran into an old friend from my days in Kansas City. It was wonderful to see his face. We hugged, and as we did, he gave me a sweet kiss on the cheek—not an uncommon gesture between us. As we sat down and got caught up on what had happened since our last visit, I was reminded of when I first met him and how I'd grown to love him.

We were both serving on the pastoral staff of a large church in Kansas City where we were deeply involved in the lives of many people, thus leading very busy lives of our own. We enjoyed each other's company but never really became close enough to feel any great mutual affection. He probably would have said the same about me that I would have said about him: "He's a great guy. Don't know him well, but I think I'd probably like him."

As time passed, we found ourselves involved in the same youth ministry. Through this ministry, we were invited to travel to Columbus, Ohio, to speak to a group of young adults. We would have flown, but because of how many kids from our church wanted to come along, we had to drive instead.

So, the kids piled into the van, the two of us climbed in the front seats, and we took off. I was a bit nervous, knowing that a twelve-hour journey lay ahead of us and hoping we would have something to say for at least a chunk of that time. If we didn't, it was going to be a long trip.

We started out with the usual small talk, but after a while, we began to ask each other more personal questions. Soon, we were deep in conversation about our life journeys. I shared part of my story, and then he shared part of his. We went back and forth, not just on the way to Columbus, but also on the return trip to Kansas City.

When we returned home, we both admitted that something had happened within each of us. Something unexpected. We no longer just enjoyed each other's company; there was now a new and profound love that we both felt for each other. In the sharing of our stories, we had seen the heart of the other person and had fallen in love with who that person was. Those stories were the foundation of a love that is still alive and healthy today!

And that's why this book is a *story*, not an exegesis, of God's love. Aware of both the myriad books already printed about the love of God and the vast number of wonderful theologians in the church, I wanted to make my book one that would unveil the affection of God through stories—stories that I am intimately familiar with because they are the stories I have lived through.

Jesus chose to reveal Himself and His Father not just through His actions but also through the words of the parables He told. He was the master storyteller, and He wants to use the stories of our lives to continue telling the world about His great love and affection.

At the end of this book is a section of discussion questions corresponding to the individual chapters. These questions can be used for either individual reflection or group conversation. My hope is that they will help steer you into a greater understanding of God's heart and ways.

My prayer is that, as I share my story, you will fall in love again—more deeply—with the One who made you so that He could love you. There is only one you, and His love for you is uniquely made with you in mind. That's why our individual stories are so important. Like snowflakes or fingerprints, no two are the same. Therefore, within every God story is a new facet and unique perspective of God's nature and heart.

May you find His heart for you within my story and, through it, fall ever more in love with Him. The wild love of God awaits you. Enjoy the journey!

PART ONE:
LIFE WITH MY FATHER

DAVID'S STORY

This year's Fourth of July gathering at my dad's house would be different. It had to be. I had something very specific to say to him. I didn't know how I would say it; I just knew this wasn't about me. This was about me giving my dad a gift—the gift of forgiveness. A gift with absolutely no strings attached.

Giving him this gift would mean that I could not craft my words to manipulate the moment, at least not in a way that would give me the sense of restoration that my heart so desperately needed. It had to be unconditional.

Dad had always loved gardening, especially in his later years. It had become a point of contact for us (and for anyone else he could pull into the backyard to show off his garden). So, there we were, standing at the garden's edge, just twenty yards or so from the back deck. As we stood side by side, I sensed the presence of Jesus. It felt like He was right there beside me, reminding me that I wasn't doing this alone. And that was something I needed to know.

If it weren't for the war, my dad probably would have gone to college right out of high school. Instead, like so many others, he joined the military. I never could figure out why he chose the Air Force, though. He was afraid of heights. He hated to fly. I laugh whenever I pull out one of the letters he sent to his mother in 1944. I can almost see him as a skinny nineteen-year-old kid, taking a gulp from a bottle of "pop," as he called it, while writing, "Gee, Mom, I've met some swell guys here." He actually did write that. He used the word "swell."

He was in love with a girl back home named Mary Kay Murphy. In one of his letters to his mother, he wrote, "I hope to be a family someday, if Mary Kay will have me."

Mary Kay would one day be my mom. But when my dad was writing those letters, she hadn't yet given him much hope of a future together. Even so, Dad was already writing to Mary Kay's mother, Marjorie Murphy, and calling her "Mom."

"God's Country" is what Dave DuPré called his place "back home." Thoughts of Ogdensburg, New York—a small town along the St. Lawrence River—probably took his mind to the pastime he loved most: fishing. There were pike and there were muskies, but how he most of all loved fishing for those small-mouth bass! On those days, his dad, who could otherwise be hard on the boys, was jovial and carefree. "Hardworking" and "Irish Catholic" were the two terms people most used to describe his parents. Despite their French surname, DuPré, the patriarchal family line was a long Irish one.

There were five DuPré kids: the oldest, a girl, was my aunt Jane, followed by four boys who were close, and not only in terms of age. They had a saying between them that expressed it well: "If one of us has a dollar, we all have a quarter." They lived by that motto. When the oldest brother graduated from high school, the younger ones got part-time jobs to help put him through college. They did the same thing until all four brothers had graduated from college.

Pete, the oldest of the boys, had been the first to enlist. He was in the army, stationed in Europe. Dad's younger brother Paul was in the South Pacific. Before long, he would become the South Pacific Marine Corps' gold-medal boxing champion of his weight class. Tom was too young to enlist, so he, along with Jane, did their best to handle things at home and tried not worry too much about their brothers.

I have a picture taken in 1944 of my father as a young second lieutenant leading a group of soldiers. In it, a couple dozen young men are walking perfectly in sync with their right legs out, while my dad proudly leads them, his left leg sticking out like a sore thumb. He'd lost his step while the group was turning, and the photo was snapped before he could get back into step with his men. His buddies hung the picture on the wall of the mess hall. You had to find fun somewhere.

Dad turned twenty in June 1944. With his chiseled face and square jaw, he could have played the dashing male protagonist in a classic 1940s romance movie. But this was no movie, and Dad had no time for romance. He had been trained as a bombardier and assigned to the United States Eighth Air Force, based in southern England, a member of a B-17 crew that would fly across the English Channel and participate in strategic bombing campaigns against industrial and military targets. The crew's primary duty was carpet bombing certain areas to create a path of less resistance for the Allied ground troops who were fighting their way east across occupied France and into Germany.

In his earliest missions, Dad sighted targets and dropped bombs. When I was a little kid, I once asked him if he had killed anyone during the war. His face darkened, and he pulled back from me before saying, "I was a bombardier. I'm sure I did." Then he turned and quickly walked away. I never pressed him on the issue again.

After his sixth mission or so, he was sent back to the States to learn how to use this new thing called radar, which promised to improve the accuracy of bombing, especially on cloudy days. Then he rejoined his crew as the "radar man"—a position that also put him in charge of making sure his fellow crew members in the back of the plane got out safely if anything happened. The crew at the front was the responsibility of the captain.

It was a sunny day on January 14, 1945, when my father and his squadron loaded into their tired-looking but very reliable B-17G, their "home away from home" as they called it. He was a member of the 838th Squadron, 487th Bombardment Group, 3rd Division of the 8th U.S. Army Air Force, and very proud of it. As he said to me a number of times, "We loved England, but it was always so much better to land there after a mission than to take off from there for one."

He was on his thirteenth mission when a new set of orders came in. The squadron was to keep heading east, right into Germany. Occupied France was no longer the final destination, it was now time to push into Germany. The Allied Forces were moving toward Berlin, which necessitated initial bombing runs into Germany.

Unbeknownst to the B-17 squadrons, heavy German artillery guns were waiting for them at the border. When Dad's squadron crossed into Germany, the big guns below swung into position to take down one Allied bomber after another. The B-17 shook violently as Allied planes began exploding on all sides.

Soon, the sky was filled with enemy aircraft. Within a matter of minutes, the quiet hum of B-17s sneaking into enemy territory had turned into absolute mayhem. Guns were going off. Planes were exploding. Smoke and flack filled the sky. My dad's plane was hit, and the crew knew they would soon be going down.

When a B-17 was no longer able to function in formation, its pilot would remove the plane from the group and try to maneuver the aircraft away on its own. Despite a pilot's best efforts, however, that was usually the kiss of death. When my dad's plane detached from the group, it was met by a horde of German Messerschmitts—small yet effective fighters. My dad and his fellow crew members didn't have a chance.

Knowing his time was short, my dad stood up to check on his best buddy, who was the plane's turret gunner. When Dad was upright, a piece of shrapnel ripped through his mask and stuck the mask to the inner wall of the plane. Had he still been seated, the shard would have gone through his head. He would later recall feeling as if God had saved him.

After ripping off the rest of his shredded mask, Dad went to check on his friend. Finding him hunched over, my father lifted him up to see how badly he had been hit. What he saw would be burned into his memory for the rest of his life. His friend's head was almost completely severed from his neck.

Rushing to the front of the plane, my dad found the port gunner slumped over. He realized that his friend was unconscious, but he couldn't manage to rouse him. Without hesitating, he held onto the gunner's rip cord and pushed him out of the plane, deploying the parachute. Incredibly, the man survived.

A couple of other men from the plane parachuted out until my father and the pilot were the only ones left on board. They gave each other a thumbs-up, as if to say, "Everyone's taken care of on my end," and then they both jumped out. Three seconds after my father's exit, the plane exploded. In under a minute, God had saved my dad's life, not once, but twice.

As my father was falling, an explosive wave thrust him away from the plane before gravity took its hold and plunged him into a rapid free fall toward the earth. Months of training had engrained into the men when best to pull the rip cord. Whenever a plane took off or landed, the pilot would always yell, "Fifteen hundred" when the aircraft reached the fifteen-hundred-foot elevation, to reinforce to all on board what that looked like. If you pulled the cord too late, you were likely to meet with injury or even death from hitting the ground too hard. But if you pulled it too early, you'd make yourself an easy target for flying shrapnel or guns on the ground.

Once my dad had dropped to what he thought was fifteen hundred feet, he felt around for the rip cord. It was not there. He searched frantically and found it on the opposite side of where it should have been. He would later say that he learned a very valuable lesson that day: "Never, ever, under any circumstances, put your parachute on upside down."

The moment he pulled the rip cord, the parachute whipped him around until his feet were above his head, tearing his arm muscle away from his shoulder. He fought through the pain while struggling to get his feet below his head before he hit the earth. When he finally pulled himself through the parachute cords, he saw wetlands beneath him, so he directed his chute toward a field. Floating a little closer, he realized it was a cornfield. But it wasn't just any cornfield; it was a field of cut corn. Anyone who was raised in farm country knows that a field of cut corn might as well be a field of swords sticking straight up in the air. For a kid, the swords are fun to play with. For a man hanging from a parachute, they mean something a little different.

Suddenly, Dad spotted a small area without corn. When he realized the reason why—it turns out that corn doesn't grow on boulders—it was too late. All he could do was turn his body to minimize the point of contact with the rock. His right leg took the brunt of the impact and broke in nine places.

Here he was, on German soil, with a severed shoulder muscle and one leg broken like an accordion. Knowing he needed to take cover, he dragged himself to a nearby hedgerow. He hunkered down in the middle of the bushes, laid his gun across his chest, and fell unconscious.

When he came to, a young teenage girl was kneeling over him and shaking him. He heard her voice before he was alert enough to do what comes naturally to a soldier who is startled out of unconsciousness. He admitted later that if it had been the enemy, he wouldn't have had enough strength to lift his gun, let alone fire it. Through the fog in his head, he heard her say, "Parlez-vous français?"

A groggy "No" was his answer.

She then said, "Sprechen Sie deutsch?"

"No," he said again.

Finally, she asked him, "Do you speak English?"

"Yes, yes," he replied, and then blacked out again.

The young woman left him but soon returned with several men who, to Dad's great relief, appeared to be townspeople rather than the police or German soldiers. As the men carried him to a nearby farm, they told him that they were part of the French underground—the French Resistance, who were dedicated to sabotaging the Germans in every way possible. My father had landed near Brandenburg, Germany, just west of Berlin. This was not a safe territory to parachute into, and yet he landed in the midst of the kindest people he could have imagined.

The members of the Resistance did their best to treat his injuries, but they did not have the necessary medication. When they explained that his leg would surely become gangrenous and have to be amputated unless he got some antibiotics, he agreed to be turned over to the Germans, who had a reputation for respecting Allied officers enough to treat their injuries.

The Germans transported him to an old warehouse complex in Berlin where low-level medical professionals treated several hundred American and British officers. The constant fear loomed that Allied forces might bomb the complex at any moment because it appeared, from above, to be a storage facility for artillery and supplies. Unlike the clearly designated hospitals where German military personnel were being treated by the best physicians and nurses available, no signs or symbols had been put on the complex's rooftop to notify Allied bombers that the site was being used to treat the wounded—including POWs.

My dad's doctor told him, "Because you're an officer, we are taking good care of you. Then you will be transferred." In other words, they were getting him healthy enough to move to a German prison camp.

The buildings on the site formed the shape of the letter H. My dad's room was located in the lower right-hand "leg" of that H. One night, Dad was jarred out of slumber by a series of explosions. He took cover as the wing that made up the middle portion of the H was completely bombed out, and a large section of the building directly across from him was demolished.

The portion of the building where he was huddled shook wildly from the explosions, but didn't erupt. As dawn approached, he looked outside and saw why: just twenty yards from his window, an unexploded American bomb was embedded in the ground with its tail sticking up in the air. It had never gone off. He felt that his life had been miraculously spared for a third time. *Somehow, for some reason, God wants me to live,* he thought. That belief, and the confidence it engendered, would keep him going through the harsher times ahead.

Before the war, my dad's faith in God had been more of a communal thing. Church was a very important part of the life of his Catholic family, and they attended mass every Sunday. His parents demanded that their children honor God and the Catholic Church. But as he lay on that bed in the German hospital, his faith in God suddenly became much more personal.

When he was "healed enough," he was transferred to one of the Stalag Lufts, Nazi prisoner-of-war camps known for their cruel treatment of Allied prisoners. Because Allied "flyboys," the American and British airmen, had inflicted the most damage to his cause, Hitler encouraged harsher and harsher treatment toward them as the war continued. Hitler had recently made a decree concerning the Allied flyboys that gave the guards at Stalag Luft greater liberty in their abuse and ill-treatment of the airmen. Hollywood sometimes gives us a glossed-over version of prison life as a POW, but my father would never romanticize anything from his time in the camps.

It was early 1945, and the war was ticking down. The German forces were getting desperate for replacements for their wounded and deceased soldiers, which meant that hotheaded boys between the ages of twelve and fifteen were handed rifles and tasked with guarding prisoners at the camps. One young Nazi guard, who had probably been in the Nazi youth movement, had it in for my dad right away. He resented my dad for having received decent care in a hospital while sick or injured German soldiers were not receiving the treatment they needed, and he exacted revenge in a number of ways, including regularly slamming my dad in the head with his rifle as they passed in a corridor.

Maintaining hygiene was impossible. Any extra water to wash faces and bodies was sloshed in a trough outside the barracks, to be used by all the men. Men would sit around picking lice off one another like monkeys in an effort to ease their constant discomfort.

Dad's prison cell was dark and so dank, it was hard to breathe. Every meal consisted of a mush made from grain, rutabaga, and water, and served in portions just large enough to keep a man alive. If the prisoners did get a slice of bread, it was usually covered with sawdust or mold. Because bread was usually just thrown into the barracks, they had to learn how to work together to make sure that each prisoner received his fair share. This one little act of cooperation produced a bond between the men that became one of my dad's greatest joys.

Overall, Dad remained close-lipped about the details of his time in prison for the rest of his life. I would try to pry more information from him, but I couldn't get him to tell me anything beyond generalities. He did say that the officers were the only Germans who weren't abusive, and that his comrades there were amazing men who deserved the highest of honors.

The only other thing he often mentioned was that he never, ever wanted to eat another rutabaga. Daily servings of rutabaga soup for months on end would make me feel the exact same way.

As the Allies steadily pressed forward into Germany, my dad and the other prisoners were moved from one location to another. Sometimes, they were kept in old warehouses; other times, their quarters were nothing more than a hole in the ground. The prisoners knew the war was coming to an end when the guards toned down their abuse, obviously unwilling to anger the prisoners if their roles were soon to be reversed.

A small number of prison guards voiced thoughts of executing the prisoners in the final hours before the camp was abandoned, but that did not happen. Instead, General Patton and his troops liberated the camp, and my dad was transported to a house where ex-prisoners recuperated before going back home.

Before being shot down, my father would never have thought he'd enjoy eating his tasteless K-rations, the prepared military meals that were given to each soldier. But as a newly freed man, he devoured them like they were the finest Thanksgiving meal he'd ever had. He was feeling very blessed to be breathing and out of the prison camp. But no one yet knew he was still alive.

At this time, his brother, my uncle Pete, was stationed in Europe. He had heard that my father was missing in action, but no one knew if he was dead or alive. While he certainly hoped that my dad was still alive, Uncle Pete had little faith he'd ever see my dad again. Having recently been promoted from Corporal to Sergeant, Uncle Pete was sitting at his desk, going over papers from his day's activities, when the phone rang. He picked up, and the caller asked, "Is this Corporal DuPré?" My uncle, proud of his new rank, promptly corrected him: "No, this is Sergeant DuPré." The caller replied, "Well, this is Lieutenant DuPré."

To my uncle, there was only one Lieutenant DuPré: my father, Dave DuPré—and he was missing in action and presumed to be dead. My uncle hesitated a few moments before replying. "Listen," he said, "I don't know who you are, but you need to know that's not funny at all!"

Without missing a beat, my father quietly said, "Pete, it's Dave." With that, my father began his journey home.

2

THE RETURN OF A WAR HERO

Ever since arriving at my dad's house earlier that day, I had been looking for an indication of how he might receive what I planned to share. I knew that my saying "I forgive you" would imply that there was something to forgive and might provoke a hostile or defensive response. In order for my gift to be unconditional, it would have to be given with no fear of his probable reaction.

There was already a crowd at the house. I went looking for my dad and found him in the backyard, surveying his garden. As I stepped onto the back porch, he turned, and we locked eyes. Sensing God's presence, I knew this was the window of time for me to say what I needed to. And so, I headed in Dad's direction.

⌒

Dave DuPré came home from the war a hero. Even using crutches, and with a full cast on his right leg, he looked so smart in his uniform that Mary Kay Murphy took a second look at him. At every turn, someone was saying to her, "You would be an idiot not to marry him. He's going to be a teacher here, and come on, he's so handsome. You two would have such beautiful children together."

What she didn't realize was that the "aw shucks" Dave DuPré who'd been "like family" before the war had returned a different person. And she had no way of predicting that, before long, she would begin to see two different Daves—the Dave from before the war and the Dave altered by the war. So when this war hero who had been a longtime family friend asked her to marry him, she thought, *Well, my mom already loves him, and this is what girls my age do, isn't it? Sure!*

A year after the wedding, a baby girl came along. They named her Carol. She was a redhead with all the redheaded traits: cute, energetic, and full of spit and vinegar. Six years later, Mark was born. A blood disorder kept him in the hospital a lot. He was physically weak and had to be watched over vigilantly. Dad really didn't know what to do with him, so he pulled away, physically and emotionally. A year later, I was born, strong and healthy, but Dad remained distant and withdrawn.

After going back to college to earn his teaching certificate, Dad became a high-school teacher of his favorite subject: history.

He taught in the same K-12 school my siblings and I attended, and when I started kindergarten, I got my first glimpse of him in his classroom. It took me by such surprise that I stopped dead in my tracks. I'd had to stand on tiptoe to see through the window on the door, and I'm sure my mouth was hanging open and my eyes bulging. I might even have been shaking my head back and forth as I thought, *Who is this man? I don't know him.*

He was sitting on the edge of his desk, looking as comfortable as could be. He was smiling and laughing, and the "huge" tenth graders in his class were smiling and laughing right back at him.

Even more shocking, as I was walking down the hall, one big kid after another would say to me, "Hey, Mr. DuPré's your dad, right? Wow. He's my favorite teacher." It seemed that he was everybody's favorite teacher. At five years old, my little brain just couldn't get around it. This popular teacher was not the man I knew from home. I had seen him acting happy when we'd gone fishing with his brothers, but it was strange to see him in a good mood surrounded by kids.

At home, his good mood never surfaced, but his irritation sure did. I didn't know that fathers were not supposed to hit their kids. I knew a couple of other kids whose dads hit them, too. I just assumed that a slap from dad was an everyday occurrence for every child, and that when dads were really mad, well, anything was possible.

One day during my first week of kindergarten, I was pulled out of class and summoned to my dad's class. Standing at about three-and-a-half feet tall, I felt very small in the big world known as the "high school wing." Timidly, I knocked on the door; the sound echoed eerily in the empty hallway. From behind the massive door, I heard my dad say, "Come on in."

The door creaked as I opened it. There stood my dad, all the way across the silent room, grinning from ear to ear. I wasn't smiling, though. I stood frozen in the doorway.

"Chris," he said, his voice unnaturally cheery, "stand right here."

I moved in cautiously and stepped to the spot he was pointing to. It was dead center, right up in front of thirty or so kids who, even sitting down, were taller than I.

"Chris, say the names of the presidents—in order, of course."

This request was nothing new. By the time I was four, I was able to recite the names of all the US presidents in order—something Dad had taught me. So, I went ahead and named them aloud, starting with George Washington and ending at Dwight D. Eisenhower. (It *was* 1959, after all.)

"Thank you, Chris," my dad said. "You can go back to your *kindergarten* class now."

The way he emphasized "kindergarten" made me believe that he was proud of my ability. It was flattering to think that he wanted his whole class to know that his son could do something that other kindergartners couldn't do.

Only later did I realize why his students had burst into moans and groans as I left the room. Prior to summoning me, my dad had announced to his students his expectation that they would be able to list the presidents in order before the end of the first month of school. Of course, the students groaned, "We have to learn *all* the presidents by the end of the month? That's just too hard!" He then walked over to the little telephone hanging on the wall of his room. His mannerisms told the class, "Well, it's all of you who are *forcing* me to do this," as he picked up the little phone and called my classroom.

"Chris, your dad wants you," said my teacher.

I was summoned to his classroom two more times that week, since my dad taught three sections of American History classes. At this point, I still thought my time to shine had really come—that my dad was finally proud of me. And so, I dutifully recited the presidents to all his classes, as a kindergartener and the following year, too, as a first grader.

I didn't understand until the next year why his students had suddenly stopped being nice to me in the halls and instead would poke me or hit me with their books whenever they saw me. He was using a five-year-old to show them up and prove his point.

When I reached second grade, I looked at my dad and saw that it wasn't me he was proud of. He was proud of himself. That was the last time I recited the presidents in order in front of his class. The next time he summoned me to do it, I made up an excuse, saying I didn't feel well. In reality, I just felt used. I felt like he was setting himself up to look good through me. And, without knowing it, he was also setting me up to be disliked and bullied by the older kids.

By this time, I was no longer confused by the difference between the man I knew from home and the man I saw at school. The way I figured it, the one at home hit me with his hands; the man at school hit me with the smile on his face. At age seven, I was stronger and more physically active than my older brother, and my sister, Carol, was now a teenager, so I became Dad's constant target.

The physical injuries my dad had sustained in the war had long since healed, but the psychological stress damage was another story. People didn't talk about post-traumatic stress disorder back then—I'd never even heard the term—but my dad was a textbook case. He treated the effects of what had happened to him the same way he treated anything he didn't want to deal with: by stuffing them out of sight.

He did the same thing with the household bills that came in. Mom was always finding unopened bills in the back of his dresser drawers or stuffed inside shoe boxes on the floor or the top shelf of his closet. He was so overtaken with fear when he looked at a bill that he just wouldn't pay it. Instead, he'd come looking for me.

Unpaid bills were the reason we kept having to move from place to place. By the time I turned eight, we had lived in nine different homes. Eventually, I stopped storing my clothes in my dresser. I would just lay them on my bed or over a chair. *Why bother?* was my thought. *We'll be moving soon.*

Dad was verbally abusive almost all the time, and I was always on the lookout for signs that it was about to escalate to something physical. I'd listen carefully for his car to pull up to our house after work because I could predict his mood by how he slammed his car door. If the slam was abrupt and hard, I did my best to avoid him.

If I heard my dad walking down the hall, I would hide in my room until I heard him move to another part of the house. The last thing I wanted to do was put myself where he could get an easy whack at me.

Predicting his behavior wasn't always possible, though. Even when a day seemed to be going along okay, things could suddenly shift. This uncertainty kept me constantly on edge. I never knew if I would be hit or just yelled at if I said something in a way he didn't like or asked him a question he didn't want to answer. Over and over, I would let my guard down just a little when things started to calm down, only to have Dad turn on me again. He seemed to enjoy smacking his kids in the back of the head for no reason.

I learned the basics of physics—force, speed, and velocity—when I was four years old. I found out that when a grown man forcefully pushes you away, you first hit the floor really hard, and then you slide with great speed across the room until you come to an abrupt stop against the wall. The bruises from Dad's blows blended right in with the bruises I got from collisions with the ground or with branches while I was playing or climbing trees, which made it easy for me to explain them away when people asked.

One time, I had to work extra hard at covering up several large bruises Dad had given me. We were living in an aging house at the time with barely any insulation that my siblings and I dubbed "the old stone fort." It was always freezing cold, and it didn't help that Dad often forgot to pay the heating bills. Before going to bed, we'd clothe ourselves in as many layers as possible before bundling blankets on top of ourselves.

When Mom asked me about these particular bruises, I mixed truth with fiction, thanks to the cold snowy weather. I told her that I'd been sledding with our dog, Prince, in a box that had hit a bunch of rocks. I knew the bruises in question weren't really from my box-sled ride with our big German shepherd, but I presented her with a very convincing case. She could see the rocks in the snow, and the box had pretty much fallen apart by that time, so she seemed to believe my story.

There is a big difference between discipline and violence. In my case, it was not a matter of a father disciplining his son or spanking him because of some wrong he had committed. It was not born out of love, and it was not connected to any misbehavior on my part. For Dad, it was a violent eruption of pent-up stress and emotion. For me, it was a life of enduring regular verbal abuse, getting whacked at random, and being hit severely every once in a while.

I don't want to paint a picture of a horrible childhood. The truth is, there were good moments here and there. But even amid the good moments, and definitely during all the other ones, I was constantly on edge, walking on eggshells and acutely aware of where Dad's hands were when I was around him.

I don't think my mom was fully aware of the extent of Dad's abuse, but she must have known that he hit me. One time, when I was six or seven, she laid into him right in front of me after seeing him give me a whack. She intervened on other occasions, as well, getting him to back off.

Even so, I never saw my parents fight with each other. Their coexistence in the same household was polite and civil—very businesslike. At the time, I didn't think it was unusual that I never saw them kiss, hug, or display any other signs of affection. I didn't know any better. When I was older, I learned that they had separated two or three times before I was even conceived.

They might have stayed together as long as they did out of a sense of obligation instilled in them by the Catholic Church. Our family was very involved in the local parish; my mother taught catechism to the senior-high students, my dad read from the Scriptures and helped collect the offering at mass, my sister sang in the choir, my brother played the organ, and I served as an altar boy. We were committed, that's for sure.

We were also in survival mode as we moved from house to house, and it was easy to see that Mom's patience with the situation was wearing thin. Rather than trying to explain what was going on with Dad, she would encourage me by saying things like, "It's not always going to be like this," and "We are going to be okay."

My mother was an amazing woman. During the war, she joined the Women's Army Corps (WAC) and learned how to fly a plane. She was such a skilled pilot that she became a top flight instructor at the military base, until an insecure military leader determined that women shouldn't be teaching men to fly, at which point Mom was suddenly reassigned to perform secretarial duties.

I had seen pictures of her wearing a pilot's uniform and standing alongside an airplane, and I knew there was more to her than a submissive wife who quietly bore her husband's oppression. At one time, she had been very independent. She made it a point to convey to me, in numerous ways, her desire to make a better life for me.

The change came when I was eight years old. It was the summer of 1962, and our family had made a safe landing at my grandmother's house in downtown Rochester, New York, after being forced to leave yet another place we had called home for a very short time. One day, home from shopping, Mom walked in the back door at the exact moment my dad knocked me off my feet and sent me flying into a wall. As I tried to catch my breath, my eyes locked with my mother's, and she looked at me in a way that said, *I am here to protect you.*

Shortly after that incident, we vacationed with some extended family along the St. Lawrence River. Unlike the two-week trips we'd taken there in the past, we went for the entire summer, and my mother had come along.

Everyone seemed to be on edge. My siblings and I had fun with our cousins, but things felt very different from any prior trip. It turned out that during this time, my mother was making plans for our departure when the summer was over. At the end of our vacation at the river, Dad headed back to Rochester; Mom and we kids headed to Marion, thirty miles away.

I realize that our move to Marion was a much bigger issue than just what I had been going through. My personal hardships were just one small piece of a larger picture. However, it seemed to me, at the tender age of eight, that my mother had somehow cantered in on a white horse and saved the day. She did what was needed for us and for herself. After we moved, I felt safe for the first time.

In the tiny house Mom set up for us in the small town of Marion, New York, life was stable and peaceful. Every day was basically like the one before it. When I returned home from school, Mom would be waiting in the kitchen. My siblings and I played games or sat on the couch and watched movies together. Of course, my brother and I fought, as all brothers do; and I thought my sister was a stupid teenager. But we were safe. Life had an easy, normal flow. We followed a predictable routine. I knew what to expect and could finally rest and relax in my own home.

Until he was able to secure his own apartment, Dad stayed at the home of my maternal grandmother. Manu, as we called her, remembered the man he'd been before the war and wanted to do what she could to help him. Without any family responsibilities weighing on him, he was free to focus on his teaching and was better able to handle the administrative side of teaching. But whenever we got together with him, his moods were still volatile; he was either surly or uncomfortably nice. We never knew which Dad to expect.

3

IN MY FATHER'S HOUSE

The happy voices and laughter of our loved ones chatting and catching up behind us on the back deck gave me some reassurance that my dad wouldn't hit me upside the head when he heard what I was about to say. As a child, I had always paid close attention to where his hands were. Now, here I was, a grown man with a wife and children of my own, and yet I was still paying attention to every movement of his hands. I was still in hyper-alert mode, ready to duck or back away, if need be, even though he was entering the end of middle age, and I was in my prime.

The risk that afternoon wasn't, in reality, a physical one. I knew that. The possibility of him verbally exploding, though, loomed large. Although our relationship ran only as deep as the reciting of current events in our lives, it was something I valued greatly and didn't want to lose. Contemplating the possible loss of this fragile connection to my father brought back memories of the time long ago when I had taken a similar risk.

M y dad's day to visit was Sunday. My brother almost always found something else to do and my sister would invariably jump in the car and take off, but I was too young to come up with any excuses and frequently had to stay indoors with Dad. All he usually did was watch football or baseball—the Cleveland Browns or the New York Yankees. My friends would be outside playing, but there I was, Sunday after Sunday, stuck inside, sitting on the living room floor, while my dad was sprawled out asleep on the couch.

My dad was at his best during our summer family vacations at the St. Lawrence River. He loved spending time with his brothers and their families, and he loved fishing. There were times when he would be "just like a regular dad." In fact, anytime we spent the day with one or more of his brothers, I would see a gem of a man all day long. During those times, I could understand why his students loved him. I would catch glimpses of greatness in this man I usually feared. But that greatness disappeared when we were back inside the four walls of the house. I had no way of understanding back then that, in many ways, he was still in that prison camp—and we were there with him.

When I was a student in high school, sports were my only real connection point with my dad. The track and field were a fair distance from the bleachers, but at least it was something. I fell into a performer/spectator relationship with him, for a number of reasons. For one thing, I was naturally athletic; sports came easily for me. For another thing, I had seen my parents dote on an athletic young man named Jake.

Jake was sixteen when he and his foster brother, Owen, came to live with us for a few years. I was four or five. In the midst of all their marriage problems, maybe my parents hoped that by helping two boys whose families had fallen apart, they could prevent their own family from doing the same.

Owen caused some havoc in our home before he left to join the Navy, but Jake...well, Jake was my hero. For the time that he was with us, he was the king of our home and even the king of our town. Small towns make heroes of standout athletes, and Jake was a basketball star. My mom became Jake's second mother, and my dad handled him with kid gloves. Seeing Jake get the royal treatment while my dad treated the rest of us so abrasively was horrible. But that didn't stop me from loving Jake. He let me come into his room whenever I wanted to. He'd tell me about his day at school and describe in detail one of the many shots he'd made to win a game.

It was a dream to have a local celebrity living in my house and treating me like his kid brother. But the more I came to love and look up to this larger-than-life figure, the more it stung to see my dad treat him like a prince. It only made it worse that Jake treated me so well. My foster brother became so important to me that after I'd gone almost ten years without seeing him, I broke down when I saw his silhouette in the door of the church on my wedding day. The sun was behind him, so I couldn't see his face at all, but I knew it was Jake. I ran straight into his arms, weeping. His presence that day meant everything to me. He had his shortcomings, but he loved me well. Jake was one of the men God brought into my life along the way who helped me to see that not all males are untrustworthy.

Like every high-school athlete, I approached my senior year expecting glory. The year before, as a junior, I had been seeded first in my district as the top triple jumper. The sectionals were held in Hornell, a small town in southern New York. I was also seeded first in the 440, a race that's one lap around the track—a distance of four hundred and forty yards. (Today, it's known as the 400, since track and field events are now measured according to the metric system.)

At the qualifying event for the state meet, held near New York City, I was expected to win both events. I kept a close eye on the other top track athletes from my state, and I knew my race times and jump distances were equal to or better than the competition. That meant I would be going to nationals, if everything went according to plan.

A lot was riding on this track meet in May of 1971. I had received letters from schools with some of the top track teams in the country. There was a good chance that William and Mary and possibly Villanova would offer me a partial scholarship or possibly even a full ride—room and board, tuition, and books— if I stayed healthy and kept up a consistent track career.

I was very excited that day because I expected to win both events. It wasn't a matter of pride; it's just what the numbers said. I easily won the first 440, which qualified me to run in the finals later that day. I watched the other qualifiers run, and the closest time to mine was about five seconds slower—a significant difference in a race like the 440.

After the qualifying races were done, I went over to the triple-jump pit to get my mark and do some practice jumps.

Something about the pit looked wrong. I took out my tape and measured. Sure enough, the distance from the takeoff board to the end of the pit was too short.

I realized that I would probably overshoot the end of the pit—something I'd done once before—if I took off from the same spot as the other competitors. So, I requested approval from the officials to adjust my takeoff spot. Approval was granted.

When I was cleared for my practice jump, I assumed that someone had raked the pit. Someone had—but he'd assumed that no one would jump as far as the back of the pit.

He assumed wrong.

I had a great jump. I went almost 48 feet—one foot longer than my best jump. What happened next changed my life. My left foot landed on a rock that was submerged beneath the sand, and every tendon and ligament in my ankle burst upon impact. The ankle turned and twisted and popped so loudly that my coach heard it from over a hundred yards away. When he saw me writhing in pain on the ground, he raced over to me and asked if I was OK and whether I thought I could still run. I lifted my left foot, and we both knew the answer. My ankle was already the size of a football. We both knew that I was finished, not just for the day but for the entire season.

I could see by the look on my dad's face that he felt badly for me. He hurried over, but there was nothing he could do to change what had happened. I was rushed to a local hospital for X-rays. When the results came back, the doctor explained that no bones had been broken, but the soft tissue around my ankle was shredded. It actually would have been better, he said, to have broken the bone, as the damage done would hinder me from ever having a strong ankle again. He told me my jumping days were over. Then he put me in a soft cast, gave me a set of crutches, and sent me home. Track scouts were in the stands, but I never heard from any of them about a scholarship. The injury was life-changing in a number of ways. My ankle did get better, but the doctor was right: I would never be able to triple-jump again.

But an unexpected gift launched me into new waters. On one of his Sunday visits, my dad came in with a guitar in his hands. He said he figured I needed something to do while I was sitting at home on the couch with my ankle wrapped. The guitar looked like a "Kmart special"—lightweight and much smaller than most guitars. But that flimsy-looking instrument would lead me to a place where I would take the risk of being hurt by my dad in a different way in my search for a new point of connection with him. It would also open the door to the world of music and, one day, to a life of ministry I'd never even knew existed.

First let me explain why my dad knew I'd love a guitar. My love of music began with the Beatles. When my parents split up, in the summer of 1962, I was eight years old, and I began throwing terrible temper tantrums. Also, for the first time in my life, I was struggling in school. My mother was getting concerned.

Then the Beatles came on the scene. Their music was upbeat, fun, and infectious. I couldn't get enough of it. The effect on my soul was life-giving. When I was nine, I formed a pretend Beatles band with my brother and two of my friends, who were twin brothers. We made cutout guitars for ourselves and dressed up like the Beatles. I was John Lennon, Ricky was Paul McCartney, and Randy was George Harrison. My brother, Mark, was Ringo Starr. We would set up the speakers from the record player outside on the porch and blast the Beatles' music while we stood on the front lawn and mouthed the words to their songs. We put on quite the lip-synched, fake-guitar performance for any passersby.

I had suddenly developed an interest in music, and it wasn't long before I was singing everywhere I went—much to the chagrin of my friends. My mother used to say to me, "The Beatles helped save your soul. They gave you your heart back." It was true.

Eight years later, when my dad bought me that guitar, he might have been thinking that since Beatles music helped me so much when I was little, it might help me again. Because I loved the Beatles so much, I'm sure he thought I'd been playing their songs exclusively.

"So, have you been learning some Beatles songs?" he asked me one day.

"Well, actually, I've only been playing songs I wrote," I told him.

"Oh. Play one of those, then," he replied.

"Well, I wrote one based off the title of this book." I showed him the book. It was called *In My Father's House*. The title had prompted me to think about what it must be like in my dad's apartment, a quiet place with no one there to tell him, "I love you." From there, I had written the song by the same title.

"It's about a guy who lives alone," I added.

After a long and uncomfortable hesitation, my dad finally spoke. "Okay, let me hear it."

I had put off this moment for months. The idea of playing that song for him seemed like an awfully big risk because I felt there was a good chance of his getting mad when he heard it. *Well*, I thought, *here goes*.

I fully expected him to explode. Instead, as I played the song, its haunting melody a backdrop for the intimate lyrics, tears filled his eyes. When the song was over, he said nothing but got up and left the room. I was devastated as he proceeded to exit the house. Looking through the window, I saw him head straight for his car. As he opened the car door, I turned away. Though I was sad and disappointed, I was also relieved that he hadn't blown up.

A minute later, the front door opened, and Dad walked back into the house. I was more than a little surprised. He reentered the living room with a serious and determined look on his face, and as he headed straight for me, I noticed that he was carrying something. When I realized what it was, my breath caught in my throat. His big, strong fingers grasped a small black tape recorder.

He said, "Would you sing it one more time so I'll always have it with me?"

I put my head down and pretended to tune a string so he wouldn't see my teary eyes. After a moment, I quietly said, "Okay." Then I went through the song once more while Dad held a little plastic microphone to my mouth.

Those were the longest minutes of my life. I couldn't look at Dad as I sang, but when the song was over, I glanced over and saw that he was crying again.

We now had a new connection point, one that took us beyond sports. Through that simple song, I had communicated to him that I saw his pain and cared about it. I had given him a glimpse of the real me—a young man who was more than just an athlete—and he hadn't rejected me.

My dad told me that he'd played the song for several other people, but I was still shocked when my uncle Pete later said to me, "Yeah, your dad cries when he's driving around listening to that song." I had never really seen the tender, emotional side of my dad, so I was puzzled, yet deeply touched. "I had to listen to that song over and over again while I drove with your dad all the way up to the river," Uncle Pete added.

Years later, I would learn that during this time, my dad had been meeting with an older veteran who now worked as a professional counselor. This man was helping my father talk through what had happened to him during the war. Just as my own life was taking a turn that would eventually lead to my ministering to others, my dad was getting the help he needed that would eventually lead to his helping other veterans.

My dad's reaction to hearing the song I'd written should have clued me in that he was undergoing a change, but unforgiveness is a demanding boss. Still blinded by my own pain and lingering bitterness, I couldn't yet see the man others saw.

4

SCHOOL DAZE

Like a man facing death who sees his life flash before his eyes, I found myself filled with so many thoughts as I stood next to my dad. Well, okay—maybe it wasn't quite that dramatic. But I knew this was a pivotal moment. As we both took in the beauty of his garden, I knew one thing: in just a few minutes, things would be different, one way or another.

I was glued to the TV whenever the Olympics were on. Like millions of other kids, my dream had always been to one day compete at that level. For me, that dream was shattered along with my left ankle in the triple-jump pit. And so were my dreams of receiving a full-ride athletic scholarship to either William and Mary or Villanova. Both schools were looking for someone who excelled in very specific events in which I would never again compete.

Even so, I kept up my hopes that another school might offer me an athletic scholarship. My ankle recovered enough by my senior year that, if I taped it every day, I could play soccer. I was team captain, and our team won the sectionals that year. Winning gave me enough of an adrenaline rush to keep me from nose-diving into a state of depression. When I was picked for the first string all-county team, my hopes were high that some college would hear about me, recognize my name from track-and-field fame, and want to recruit me.

But none did.

Then, there was basketball. I had played every year growing up. That's just what you did during the winter in a small town like Marion. Virtually the entire town would show up and pack the gym for every home game. It was so intense that one man actually had a heart attack during a game and had to get a doctor's permission to attend games later in the season. In Marion, population four thousand, people were nice to you when your team won, but rude or indifferent when you lost. When we won, we won as a town. When we lost, only the players lost.

By my senior year, I'd had enough of the small-town basketball culture and decided I really didn't enjoy the game enough to be bothered by the duplicity. I played because it was what my friends and I had always done. It was either that or wrestling. The options were pretty limited.

So, during senior year, a few of us decided to create another option. Instead of signing up for basketball, we launched a volleyball team. Our German teacher, who had been on the German national volleyball team, volunteered to be our coach.

Needless to say, our plan did not go down well with the long-time basketball coach. He called me into his office one day and asked me why I wasn't playing basketball. I told him that basketball was never my great love and that I was tired of the pressure that the Marion fans put on the basketball team. It wasn't that I minded pressure or competition—I had experienced plenty of both with soccer and track. I just didn't like basketball all that much. It was my senior year, and I wanted to enjoy myself.

Suddenly, the six-foot-five-inch man, who had been my encouraging coach for years, stood up from his desk, walked around until he stood directly in front of my chair, gave me a long, intimidating gaze, and then slapped me across the face. The blow seemed to come from out of nowhere. It was so hard that it knocked me off my chair.

I pulled myself up off the floor and sat back down on the chair, stunned by what had just happened. The basketball coach started shouting, telling me how much talent I had and that I was wasting it. He added that I was influencing others to waste their talents, too, on a "stupid sport" like volleyball. "I was brought to this town to raise up a winning basketball team," he yelled, "and you're working real hard to destroy that possibility."

I raised my eyebrows at him. *And this is the way that you're inviting me back to your team?* I thought.

But all I said was, "Are we done?"

Turning away, he replied, "Yes."

I got up and walked out of there with a big red hand-shaped mark on my face. Some of my friends asked what had happened to me, but I just told them it came from a wayward blow from a rebound during gym class.

I didn't report the basketball coach to the principal. Neither did my closest friends, when I finally told them the truth. I understood…they were on the basketball team. Back then, nobody thought about suing over the things they do now. I had already learned to cover for my dad, so covering for the coach came naturally. He was just another male authority figure who taught me the consequences of failing to do what he wanted me to.

My response to the coach's anger was to forge ahead and play volleyball with everything I had. Our team ended up advancing to the sectionals. We didn't win, but, boy, did we have fun.

My last sport of that year was, again, track and field. I didn't go into a funk over my ankle, because I could still run fast even if I couldn't run the 440 or do the triple jump. I knew I'd be winning races, so I still held out hope of getting an athletic scholarship.

Halfway through the season, the track coach decided to treat one of our practices as if it were an official meet. He even brought his starting pistol with him. When he told us that we could try any event we wanted to, I decided on the low hurdles. I remembered enjoying the event when I'd tried it as a freshman.

I got into the blocks for the start. The coach was at the finish line with his stopwatch, and the assistant coach was holding the starting pistol. When the gun fired, I took off. Our team's top hurdler at the time was in the lane next to mine. He was the number three hurdler in the county and a solid athlete, but after clearing the first hurdle, I never saw him again. As I crossed the finish line, my coach let out a shout. I ran over to him, and he held out the stopwatch. I asked him if it was a good time. He stared at me and said, "You just shattered the county record."

We both agreed at that moment that I would add the hurdles to my events. I ended up breaking not only the county record but also the sectionals record. *Maybe now, some college will come running,* I thought. *Maybe now, I'll hear from someone.*

A local paper in Rochester printed a small article about me, and someone from *Sports Illustrated* even contacted my coach about the possibility of featuring me in the magazine's youth section, "Faces in the Crowd." I waited, and my coach made some follow-up calls, but nothing happened. No colleges responded.

I was devastated. Here I was, swarmed at the end of every track meet by people cheering me and even requesting autographs. I thought for sure that I would hear from someone. Anyone.

At the end of our senior year, all my friends were going off to college. My best friend, Tom, was headed to Cornell; another close friend had received an athletic scholarship to Bucknell; and my brother was returning to Holy Cross for his sophomore year. At one time, it had seemed I had a scholarship and a future. Now, I was empty-handed. Everyone else had somewhere to go, but it felt as if I was going nowhere. Looking back now, I know that God was in the midst of it all, but I didn't see it then.

I never considered the possibility of earning any kind of scholarship besides an athletic one. Labeling had blinded me to the fact that my brother, whose genius-level IQ was just a few points higher than mine, wasn't the only "smart one," and that my sister, who could captivate a crowd without trying, wasn't the only "good communicator." I knew I was a smart kid with good communication skills, but I had interpreted the label of "the athletic one" as permission to hide my insecurities in the shadow of my physical abilities. As a result, I failed to develop my God-given potential in other areas.

I had so relied on receiving an athletic scholarship that I had ignored the obvious: schoolwork. I don't say this proudly, but not once did I bring schoolwork home during my last two years of high school. When my mother asked why I never had any homework to do, I told her that it was because I had two study halls at the end of every day. That was partially true; I would often do a little homework during the pre-practice athletic study hall and then finish the remainder during homeroom the following morning, in the midst of announcements and daily attendance. I could knock out a halfway-decent, two-page book report in a twelve-minute homeroom after making a quick scan of the assigned reading. I never realized that if I would have just spent a little time studying, I probably could have earned an academic scholarship.

So there I was, or so I thought, in the race of sibling life, falling even further behind my sister, Miss Comedy, and my brother, Mr. Academics, in the sibling race. I had gone from being quite possibly one of the most self-confident teenagers around to being increasingly afraid of an uncertain future. I was no longer able to compete at the athletic level on which I had been relying for my sense of security, social identity, and future success, and it was killing me inside. Fear and deep sadness were welling up within me as it looked more and more like my future had been shredded on a rock in that unraked triple-jump pit. Of course, I kept all my feelings to myself and continued to walk out my life, now also silently suffering from constant migraine headaches. I saw no connection between the headaches and my heartache.

It also never crossed my mind to look to God for help, comfort, or answers. I viewed Him as a divine Judge who barely tolerated my existence. I figured I was on my own, keeping God's hellfire judgment at bay by faithfully attending mass every week. I didn't know that it was possible to have a personal relationship with God the Father through faith in His Son, Jesus. I didn't even know why Jesus died. The gist of what I had gathered—from my catechism classes, from the Scriptures that were read on Sunday mornings, and from comments I'd heard here and there—was that Jesus died on a cross because of my sins, and the church rituals would keep me from going to hell. I had no idea that Jesus ever thought about me and actually loved me. It never entered my mind that He wanted me to have a close, intimate, personal relationship with Him, with God the Father, and with the Holy Spirit. I didn't realize that He had died for me so that He could give me a new heart. Instead of being secure in His affection, I was chasing after His approval like I chased after the approval of everybody else.

Scholarship or not, I wanted to go to college, like most of the other guys around me, because it was the best way to avoid getting drafted into the Vietnam War. A four-year college was out of the question without either an athletic scholarship or other financial help, which I never applied for because I never thought I'd need it. So, following our high-school graduation, when my friend Mike asked me if I wanted to go with him to a community college an hour away from home, I literally went along for the ride. Together we took off to a small two-year school in Auburn, New York. At least I'd have something to do, I figured, and it would be better than going to Vietnam.

I joined the college soccer team, and even though I was a starting player, my lifelong athletic goals had been kicked to the curb. In the past, I had avoided drugs and alcohol so I could stay fit as I pursued my athletic goals. But now, with those goals forever out of reach, I saw no reason to avoid that lifestyle. I just didn't care anymore.

I still loved the game of soccer, but by the time the season was over, depression sealed me in with my new best friend—drugs. I made a bizarre pact with a friend named Bruce to get stoned every day before the day was over. In our "freedom," we decided that we would not let a day go by without getting wasted.

I was so spaced out that at the end of an entire year of school—two whole semesters—I had completed only twelve credit hours. I was often high when I was in class, and I had even more of a buzz when I was studying, which wasn't often. Some days, it was so bad that I couldn't even remember what class I had taken only hours earlier. I'd sign up for a class, then drop it because I couldn't handle it.

Toward the end of the year, I told my mom, "I just can't do school now. I don't know what I'm going to do, but I just can't do school." She could see that I was in no shape to continue as I was. When the semester ended, I packed my bags and headed home. To me, it signified another failure that confirmed what I was already feeling: I was going nowhere.

Going back home turned out to be a good move on many levels. The pressure to party every day while at school was replaced by the normal ebb and flow of family life. I continued doing drugs, but now it was just a couple of times a week instead of every day. The effort required to hide my drug habit from my mother forced me to reduce the amount and frequency I used. At the same time, a close friend from high school named Nancy had asked me to help out with her family's dairy business. They needed someone to bottle the milk two days a week and make deliveries the other three days, since her dad could no longer drive.

There's nothing like having to start work at four in the morning to help curb your drug use, not to mention all my gratitude for the appreciation Nancy's family showed me. Each workday that summer ended with the family preparing a feast for me while I lounged around by their pool. It seemed they were not just saying thanks; they were celebrating my helping them in a time of crisis. Instead of frying my brains in an effort to feel good, I was actually doing something for this family, while also providing a service to the local community.

During the summer of 1973, the drug-induced cobwebs of the past year started to clear out of my head. At the same time, my sister, my mother, my aunt, and finally my brother received Jesus into their lives. That's right—everyone at my house, and even our neighbor, became born again that summer. Everyone but me, that is. Outwardly, I joked about it, saying that our cat was probably saved, too. (The cat did seem different.) Inwardly, although I only paid halfway attention to what they were now saying, I gave my full attention to the way they were now living.

A NEW SONG

As I stood there next to my dad, my heart was warm toward him. Anytime a doubt popped into my head—like, "The last thing he wants you to do is bring up what happened in the past. Just be satisfied with what you have right now," or "You know how angry he can get. He might make a scene in front of all the family. And what about Marian and her kids? They'll all blame you for ruining such a nice day"—God's peace washed over me and silenced it.

I focused on God's presence in that moment rather than on past fears that would have held me back. My ability to feel God's presence seemed to be God's way of letting me know that this was the moment that He had been preparing *me for, step by step, year by year. In this moment of peace, I knew that all I had to do was open my mouth, and God would fill it with just the right words.*

This was not about performing or about managing my dad's reaction for my sake or others' comfort. I knew that the gift I was about to give to my father had been born out of God's gift to me.

～

My sister, Carol, had naturally curly red hair. In 1973, she puffed it out in an Afro so monstrous that, as I loved to joke, she had to turn sideways to get through a doorway. After she became a Christian, she led our mom and brother to the Lord, and then she started inviting her church friends over to the house, supposedly to visit Mom. Her real agenda, I knew, was to create a setup for her friends to talk to me about Jesus.

I saw them as people who just talked...and talked...and talked. As I waited for them to give it a rest—in other words, to shut up—I wondered how it was possible for them to say so many words in such a short period of time.

Looking back, I think they were nervous. After all, they knew they were talking to the last unsaved person in Carol's family and probably felt some pressure to get me saved. They tried to come off as normal as possible, but, in spite of their good intentions, I felt like they were putting on a show for me.

What did make an impact, however, was something my brother did. After he got saved, at the age of twenty, he gave me all his dope. Strange as it may sound, this act proved to me that his faith was real. That dope was expensive stuff, and he was just giving it away. Even though it would seem like the right thing would have been to just throw it out, God used his gesture anyway. When he handed it to me and said, "I'm not going to need this anymore," I knew for certain that my brother had been changed.

Around that time, my sister called me, wondering if I was coming to Brockport for her college graduation ceremony. I told her I was. She then asked if I could pick her up at her apartment and drive her to the ceremony. My friend Mike wanted to visit the same town, so we took off together in his car for the hour-long drive.

We smoked dope the entire way there. The car must have smelled horrible when my sister and her roommate got in.

When I had moved to the backseat and settled in beside my sister, she turned to me. "Do you remember how I used to always say, 'Someday, I'm going to be a princess'?"

"Yeah?" I answered cautiously, still feeling the full effect of the drugs.

"Well, I am."

"Ah, so you're a princess?" I asked.

"Yep."

"You got married?"

"Yep, I married a prince," she affirmed.

"And who might that prince be?"

Just as serious as could be, she said, "Jesus, the Prince of Peace."

Mike met my gaze in the rearview mirror, and our eyes locked in a silent exchange that said, *You've got to be kidding!*

"Oh, so you married the Prince of Peace?" I joked to Carol. "Was it a nice wedding?"

"Well, it wasn't really a wedding," my sister said. "We're married in my heart."

"Oh, wonderful," I said with mock enthusiasm. "I sure hope you have a nice life together."

Carol then added, "Do you know that I speak in tongues?"

"What?" I asked.

"You remember how, in church on Pentecost Sunday, we would read something about the Upper Room, and how tongues of fire came down on people, and they started speaking in tongues?"

"I think so," I replied.

"Well, I can speak in tongues."

"Okay," I said. "Then...can I hear it?"

"Oh no, it's not like that," she told me. "I'm not supposed to just say it to you like that."

With each new revelation that Carol shared with us, Mike and I exchanged glances. We could almost hear each other thinking, *Can you believe this?*

"Have you ever heard of the word 'prophecy'?" my sister asked me next.

"Yeah," I replied. "It's when people see things that are about to happen."

"Well, there is that kind of prophecy," she said, "but I mean a simple prophecy of God speaking to someone by sharing encouraging things through somebody else."

"Well, okay," I said. "What about it?"

"Well, I can speak prophetically," she declared.

"You can?" I retorted, no longer even thinly veiling the fact that I thought what she was saying was ridiculous. "So, let me get this straight. God actually speaks through you?"

"Yeah, God speaks through me," she answered matter-of-factly.

Okay, so this is how she witnesses to me? I thought. I'm stoned in the back of an Oldsmobile 442, and my sister tells me that she's married to the Prince of Peace, that she speaks in tongues, and that God speaks through her. Seriously?

"So, if God speaks through you, then what does He sound like?" I asked next.

"Well, I guess He sounds like me," she said.

"That's horrible," I stated. "God sounds like you? If God sounds like you, then I don't want anything to do with Him."

To that, she replied, "He just uses my personality and my voice."

Dying to wrap it up, I said, "I'm sorry, Carol, but that just doesn't work for me. It's awesome for you."

I had developed a habit of minimizing her latest interests because I always figured they wouldn't last long. She had been one to try new things all the time; this "Jesus thing" seemed like just another addition to a long list of hobbies and beliefs she'd sampled over the years. I assumed she would stick with it about as long as the last thing she'd been into.

Apparently not wanting to waste even a moment of the five-minute car ride to the graduation ceremony, she then said, "Have you ever heard of visions—of people having visions?"

"Maybe," I said. "Kind of. Uh...no."

"Our pastor has had visions," Carol said. "God shows him things."

"Well, that's great if God is showing people things, but I don't want your prophecy, and I don't want to speak in tongues," I told her. "If that's good for you, and you're happy, then I'm happy for you. Mike and I are happy. Aren't we, Mike?"

Mike nodded. "Yep, I'm happy."

"See, Carol? Mike's happy, and I'm happy…and we're both happy that you're happy."

Although Carol made no outward show that she'd been hurt by my mocking comments, she did stop her witnessing and instead directed Mike to the place where he could drop them off.

As Carol and her friend were getting out of the car, I told them that we would park and come inside in a few minutes. Then I got into the front seat, and when I shut the door, Mike and I busted out in hysterical laughter. He kept saying he didn't want to laugh too much, because it was my sister, but he couldn't hold it back. We both laughed so hard, our sides hurt.

My laughter did not last long, however. Mike parked the car, and as I was getting out, I heard a voice behind me say, "Everything your sister just said is true." Startled, I quickly looked around, but there was no one there. I looked in all directions, even glancing into the backseat of the car. But there was no one. Still, I was certain I had heard a voice.

"Did you hear that?" I asked Mike.

"Hear what?" he said.

Then I knew: I was the only one who had heard it.

The moment I shut the car door, I completely sobered up. The effect of the drugs should have been in my system for another hour or two, but it had instantly disappeared. Mike was still laughing and joking around, but now I was just pretending to find him funny. I couldn't get back to the high we had been sharing just moments earlier. I knew that God had physically touched me and that it was His voice that had spoken clearly and directly to me.

In the span of a five-minute car ride, my sister had told me that she had married the Prince of Peace, was now a princess, spoke in tongues, and spoke prophetically, and that the leader of her church experienced visions. No matter how offbeat and silly she had come off, a seed of truth had been planted. At that point, I knew that, sooner or later, it was going to be all over for me. I could fight it for a while, but I knew I wouldn't last. I was alone. I was alone because I was wrong. Drugs were wrong, because my brother gave them up. I started to feel absolutely certain that my days of doing things my own way were coming to an end.

My brother thought the old scare tactic might work, so he gave me a copy of the book *The Late Great Planet Earth* by Hal Lindsey. He was right. I did get a bit scared after reading a few chapters, so I decided to shelve the end-time stuff even though I knew Mark was really into it. I was in no mood to read about judgments and plagues, and yet part of me knew that there was some truth to this as well because my brother—always the analytical one—would base the decision to follow Jesus as Lord on logic and intellectual deduction. He somehow knew, then, that it was the right thing to do.

On the other hand, my sister's journey beyond the thin faith we had developed in the local Catholic parish where we'd been raised was very different. She lived in the world of emotion. She was smart—of that there was no doubt—but she had been in the middle of a personal struggle when a college acquaintance had started hounding her to turn to Jesus. This acquaintance had just gotten saved himself, and he came off as a real nuisance. But his relentless presentation of God's plan of salvation, his genuineness, and his sincere love and care for her as a person helped Carol to realize that her life really was a mess, and she really was a wreck without God's help. God plucked her out of the fire when she put her trust in Him.

Again, I suspected my time was coming, but I was still putting it off when I heard that my sister was bringing a friend to my cousin's wedding on August 18, 1973. I figured Carol and her friend would be double-teaming at the reception, trying to convince everybody there to get saved. My avoidance strategy was to sit in a corner and get drunk with my cousin.

When Carol's friend saw our isolated table as a witnessing opportunity, she asked my sister if she thought it would be a good time to share the Lord with me. By now, my sister was pretty frustrated with me for dodging her efforts at every turn, and so she discouraged her friend from even bothering to try. "I don't think Chris will ever get saved," she told her. "He always seems so happy and has great favor, so why would he see any need for turning to the Lord?"

Of course, Carol didn't know about the emptiness I felt. I was a good actor. She had no idea that the external accolades I'd received through the years had never been enough to offset how low and small I'd always felt deep down inside.

After the wedding, we headed home, and my best friend, Tom, came over. The buzz from the few beers I'd drunk at the reception had totally worn off. We were all having a good time hanging out, watching a little TV, and talking together. I left the room for a few minutes to use the bathroom and then headed to the kitchen to get something to eat. When I came back, Carol was leading Tom in a prayer to receive Jesus.

I stood there, stunned. *What is she doing?* I thought. *This is going to change everything!*

In answer to my face, which went from surprise to irritation and finally to disbelief, Tom told me, "This is real, man."

After Tom left, Carol asked me if she could tell me what she had prayed with him. I was headed to bed, so I told her she could follow me into the room. I lay down in bed, pointed to the foot of the mattress, and said, "Go ahead. Have a seat and tell me what happened."

She began to tell me, then suddenly stopped and said, "Why don't I pray with you what I prayed with Tom? If we get to a part that you don't want to say or don't believe, just don't say it. Is that okay with you?"

Smiling inwardly, I thought to myself, *Boy, is she smooth.*

By this time, it was one o'clock in the morning, and all I wanted to do was to go to sleep. But I said, "Okay," and sat up. Then I reached overhead and pulled the string to the ceiling light above us, plunging us into darkness. "Sorry," I said, to break the awkward silence. "I just don't want to do this prayer stuff with the light on. Okay, go ahead."

Carol led me in a simple little prayer—she'd speak a phrase, and I'd repeat what she said—and I believed every word of it. For as long as I could remember, I had believed that Jesus was the Son of God and that He had died for my sins. I didn't fully know what that meant, but verbalizing my beliefs in that way somehow personalized them for me.

At the end of the short prayer, I turned the light back on. I was covered in goose bumps from head to toe. "Whoa!" I said.

"Cool," Carol said.

I looked at her. "Do you mind leaving? I'd like to be alone."

"Why?"

"I just need some time alone to contemplate what I just did." I knew she probably thought that I was going to internalize what had happened and have a little prayer time of my own. But as she walked out the door, I thought, *Good. Now I can go to sleep.*

I wasn't sure what had just happened to me, but I knew one thing for certain: I did not want to confront God. He'd made me nervous in the parking lot before Carol's graduation a few months prior, and I didn't want a repeat performance. And I certainly did not want Him to show up in my bedroom. I had heard stories of God revealing Himself to people; considering Carol's bizarre testimony, I thought that if I could just get my sister out of the room and quickly turn off the light, I could keep the "God stuff" from happening.

Things went very differently, however. Right after Carol left the room, I became very conscious of Jesus, of His presence. He was no longer out there; He was within.

Jesus continued to grab my attention during the following week, surprising me with answers to even the simplest of prayers. For example, I would pray, "O God, if You could just help me," and the tractor that had been slowing me down while I was driving my dairy route would, at the exact moment of my prayer, suddenly move to the side of the road to let me pass. Or the bee buzzing around inside the truck that I hadn't been able to get rid of on my own would immediately fly out the open window. Or a parking spot in a crowded lot would open up out of the blue. I knew God was not a puppet whose strings I was manipulating, but these small miracles confirmed His desire to communicate with me, and His desire that I should communicate with Him. He was showing me that He was there. We were now in a relationship.

My relationship with God grew slowly at first. During this early stage of my new life in Him, when I had yet to be discipled, I still did drugs a couple of times. The first instance, I suffered a horrible migraine. The same thing happened the second time. When I was lying in bed, sick as a dog, I prayed, "Lord, what's going on? Why do I keep getting these migraines?"

In response to this question, a clear thought that I had come to recognize as the voice of God—the voice of truth—responded, "Those drugs are illegal, and they're bad for you." Months earlier, the same voice had told me that everything my sister had said was true. This time, when He spoke to me, I was in a personal relationship with the One who had spoken, so I was excited to hear His voice and to know His answer.

My response was, "Oh, yeah. I never thought of that. They're bad for me. So, I guess I shouldn't be doing them, should I?"

Inside, I heard a firm yet kind, "No."

"Okay. Then I'll stop." And from that moment on, I had no desire for drugs. Having heard God's message made it easy for me to put that lifestyle behind me for good.

Wow, I heard God, I thought. I was amazed, happy, thrilled, and eager to do things His way. Being in an intimate relationship with Him, knowing that He cared for every detail of my life and had my good in mind, made me feel more affirmed than ever.

A few weeks after giving my life to the Lord, I went to one of the Friday-night college services held at my sister's church in Brockport. I loved it. The people sang their hearts out during worship, and the message was relevant and even humorous at times. After the service, some friends of Carol's asked if they could pray for me. They said, "You need to be baptized in the Spirit." I said okay, and a moment later, I was surrounded by a group of about ten people touching me or extending their hands toward me. This all was pretty new to me, but I found myself going along with it.

The group began to speak in tongues, and soon I could tell that they were desperately hoping I would do the same. Every now and then, they would stop and check on me to see if I could speak in tongues yet. I couldn't, and I sure wasn't going to fake anything. Finally, after quite a while, they began to give up. The people standing on the fringes drifted away, and it wasn't long before we all knew that our prayer time was done. The remnant of people who remained encouraged me that if I kept pressing in, sooner or later, there would be a breakthrough.

I went home that night actually encouraged. I was in no hurry to have some new religious culture that I was not completely sure of be thrust upon me. The early 1970s were known as a time of great spiritual renewal in Jesus, but it was also a time of widespread counterfeit spirituality. Many cults were forming, and I had no desire to join their ranks.

When I got home, I lay down on my couch and began reading a book that someone had just given me. It was a balanced presentation of the work of the Holy Spirit. I read one chapter, then closed my eyes for just a second, fell into a deep sleep, and began to dream. In the dream, I was walking along a country road. I came to a *T* in the road. Looking right, I saw that it quickly turned into a dirt road and then, just as quickly, became a wide path that led into brambles and gnarly trees. I knew I was not to go that way. As I looked to the left, I saw a beautiful white mansion. Suddenly, an old man appeared in front of me. He was holding a sign that read "Messiah" with an arrow underneath it, pointing toward the mansion. I now knew which way to go.

When I reached the mansion, I opened the door and found that there were no rooms inside. There was just a stairway. I climbed the steps to the second floor; again, there were no rooms, only more stairs leading to the next floor. I climbed them, and there, on the third floor, the stairs ended. Before me was a round foyer about twenty feet across. On the opposite side of the foyer were two huge doors at least fifteen feet high. Standing right in front of the doors was a huge angel.

The angel had his arms folded across his chest and was looking right at me. Somehow, I knew that God was on the other side of that door, so I walked up to the angel and asked him to move. He looked down at me and said, "No." With resolve, I said, "I need to get in there." With a more serious tone of voice, he said, "You can't go in there. If you do, you will die." I then told him that I didn't care; I still wanted to go in. He gave me a slow, knowing smile and stepped out of the way.

His smile actually made me a little nervous, but I didn't care. I was going in. I walked up to the door and grabbed the handle. It was huge. I pulled, but the door didn't budge. The angel was still smiling. I gave him a quick, fake-polite smile back and grabbed the handle once more. This time, I used both hands and yanked with all my might. The door began to move, ever so slowly. It was a very thick door; I had pulled it open by at least half a foot before the inside edge of the door became visible.

Suddenly, a shaft of intense light came streaking through the crack between the doors. It was not just visible, it was tangible. It hit me, knocking me backward across the foyer. I slammed into the opposite wall and slowly sank to the ground. A moment later, the light around me began to fade, and then everything went black. I found myself back in my house, fully awake, and speaking in tongues.

I was speaking in tongues! I couldn't believe it. Then I remembered something I had just read earlier that night—that He is the one who baptizes. Now I knew it for myself.

I was now fully onboard with this new life in God. I loved it. I loved His Word, I loved worshipping with other believers, and I loved the joy that came from relationships based on life instead of drugs. I knew it was about Jesus. But something unusual would soon happen in a very dramatic way that would change my life forever.

An early official Air Force picture of my dad. He was so young and without a clue about what would soon happen.

My mother (second from left) during the war. Before being demoted by an insecure superior officer, she was not only a skilled pilot, she also taught others how to fly.

```
C A S U A L T Y       R E P O R T

Date             :     14 January 1945        Time :    1300 h
Aircraft         :     B-17G      44 - 8563
Codes            :     2C
Group/Squadron   :     487 BG   -H-   838 BS
Base             :     Lavenham, Suffolk
Crash details    :     shot down by German fighters before the
                       target. When most of the crew had bailed
                       out, the B-17 blew up in mid-air and crashe
                       at Gutenpaaren, 15 km NE of Brandenburg,
                       Germany.
Target           :     Magdeburg, Germany.
```

```
Killed : buried in the cemetery at Roskow. Reinterred in Ardennes; initial
         plot numbers between brackets.

CP   :   NYHAGEN Floyd C., 1/Lt.         O-771111  CAL
         Found on crash-site. (Z-10-233)          Ardennes D-10-39

B    :   REID Stewart F. Jr., 1/Lt.      O-773000  ILL
         Found on 17.1.45 in Feldmark              Ardennes B-38-42
         Roskow. Presumed chute failed
         partly or it was pierced by
         fighter fire. Grave 9. (AA-9-219)


P.O.W. :

P          :  STEMPLE Omar D., 1/Lt.         O-413806

N          :  CROTTY John H., 2/Lt.          O-723020

Mickey Op. :  DU PRE David J., 2/Lt.         O-696224  broke ankle

Air Leader :  REED David D. Jr., Captain     O-432109

E          :  LOY John P. Jr., T/Sgt.        34675555

RO         :  GEORGE Gust, T/Sgt.            16123280  hospitalized

BTG        :  CATHCART Charles J., S/Sgt.    33557939

WG         :  WICKMAN Norman H., S/Sgt.      36696819

N          :  HILDEBRAND Durston N., 1/Lt.   O-703255


Note: The burial of Lt. Reid in Roskow is on record. It is presumed
      that this place is also valid for Lt. Nyhagen, but not on record.

Sources: MACR. 11731
```

```
Details collected by: J.A. H e y - A.v.d.Leeuwstraat 12 - 7552 HS Hengelo
```

The casualty report of my dad's downed plane. The entry for David DuPré, third from the top, only includes a broken ankle, but my dad's actual injuries were more severe. Image courtesy of Moosburg Online, www.moosburg.org.

*My dad (right) is reunited with his
brother, my Uncle Pete, soon after
returning from Germany.*

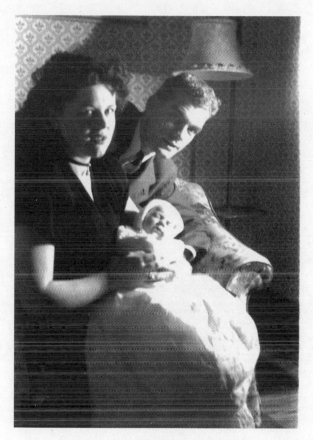

My parents with me as a newborn.

MARION BOOTERS—Comprising the Marion Central School 'ty soccer team are (front from left) Steve Delmage, Huber, Bruce Stone, Tom Haak, Gordon DePoint (co-Terry Krocke, Paul De Point, Mike Erb; (back from left) Coach Chuck Bailey, Jim Adriaansen, Karl Bueg, Tom Spittal, Chris DuPre, Howard Bush (co-capt.), Dave Sewert, John Kymble, Jay McLouth, Rafael Mella, Jim Thomas. Absent is Gary Scrooby.

In the second row, I'm standing (fifth from left) next to my best friend, Tom (fourth from left). We were saved on the same day three years after this picture was taken.

This was a proud day for me: we had just won the sectionals and it was my senior year. I'm on the far left.

PART TWO:
LIFE WITH MY NEW FATHER

6

FACE-TO-FACE

Standing there with my dad, I realized that we were not looking at each other. Instead, our gaze was straight ahead, at his garden. It was a beautiful garden, but, oh, how I longed to be able to look directly into his eyes. Maybe someday. Maybe soon. Let it be so, Lord.

S oon after being filled with the Spirit, I had another encounter with the Lord that seemed so radical, I kept it to myself for a very long time. I had moved to Brockport, New York, where my sister and brother lived. To call Brockport a college town would be an understatement. Home of The College at Brockport, the town's population doubled from eleven thousand to twenty-two thousand whenever school was in session. Young people were getting saved left and right, not just in Brockport, but all across the US. This particular era of church history would later be referred to as the Jesus Movement. We were at the tail end of it. In Brockport, every Friday night, hundreds of young people packed like sardines into a building that was intended to hold only one hundred and fifty—or, at most, two hundred. In this space, where it was almost too crowded to breathe, the lives of hundreds of kids were changed forever.

I had left my job at the dairy, since it was an hour's drive from Brockport, and I had started working at a local hospital ordering and distributing supplies. I often went back to my little second-floor apartment for lunch. The tenants living on the floor beneath me worked the night shift. They, too, were believers, and they hosted a home group at noon once a week. On the days they met, I would run home, stand over the ventilation grate in my living room, and listen in on the beautiful worship music below me as I ate my typical lunch: a bologna sandwich with mayonnaise on white bread. (It was the ultimate bachelor's meal. Not until I married my wonderful wife, Laura, did I know the kinds of food I'd been missing.)

One particular afternoon, when I was standing above the grate with my eyes closed, enjoying the music and my sandwich, I suddenly felt a breeze blow over me. I opened my eyes to check if I had left a door or a window open. What I saw was unnerving. Instead of the familiar setting of my apartment, I was now standing on a hillside. My sandwich was gone, but I was dressed in the same clothes I'd put on that morning.

I quickly took stock of the situation: I had not lain down on my bed to go to sleep, I was not high on drugs, and I was not hallucinating. I was actually standing on a hillside in the open air.

Baffled, I asked aloud, "What in the world is going on?"

The hillside was in a park, and scattered throughout the park, groups of people were picnicking together. Adults were grilling hamburgers. Kids were playing. Dogs were running around and barking. The scene was very inviting.

I then noticed several people walking by, headed up the hill, which sloped upward behind me. Somehow, I knew they were believers. As they passed me, they said, "You might as well come, because they're not listening anymore. All they want to do is eat and drink and have fun."

It was evident to me that they had just finished speaking with all the people at the picnic, none of whom wanted to hear what they had to say.

The followers of Jesus then said to me, "By the way, He's coming."

As I walked up the hill with the other believers, I wondered to myself, *What am I doing outside, walking up a hill, when I'm supposed to be in my apartment eating my lunch?*

To test the reality of the situation, I reached down, plucked a piece of grass, and ate it. It was real, all right. It tasted just like grass. I spit it out. Next, I pinched myself. Sure enough, it hurt. These two quick reality checks convinced me that something about all this was real.

It didn't take long to reach the top of the hill. There, we joined a circle of about thirty other people. They said to me, "You know He's coming soon." As we stood together and waited, I wondered if Jesus was really coming.

After a few minutes, I noticed that everyone around me was looking up. I followed their gaze and understood why. Jesus was coming down into the center of the circle as if being lowered on a cable. He wore a long robe and had bare feet. I could not see His face, as He was turned in the opposite direction. Long dark hair poured over the back of His robe.

I then thought of those poor people at the bottom of the hill who were having fun but missing out on this. My eyes were wide as I kept them fixed on Jesus and took note of His every movement. I could tell that He was now looking at those in front of Him. He gazed at each of them, one at a time.

Before long, it will be my turn, I thought. *Soon, He will be looking at me.*

Then I hesitated. *Hey, wait. He'll see everything. I don't want Him to see everything.*

I felt an urge to run. *This is not what I signed up for!* I thought. Then I realized, *But I don't want to run.*

Finally, the left side of His face came into view. His cheek was scrunched up, and His expression looked tense.

I thought, *Oh, no. He's angry!*

But when He came around so that I could see more of His face, I realized His expression wasn't one of anger at all. It was the largest smile I had ever seen!

He continued moving His gaze from person to person until, suddenly, He fixed His eyes upon me. No one had ever looked at me like that! He was looking right through me, filling every pore and every crevice of my being with light and love. The words *wild love* filled my mind and heart. Wild love! Because of His wild love, He was not constrained by anything or anyone. Nothing and no one had the power or the ability to hinder Him from loving me deeply and fully.

I could still feel His love for me when He kept on moving around the circle, looking at each person in the same way. When He was done, He got down on one knee, stretched out His hand toward us, and said, "It's time to go, My beloved. Come away with Me."

Three years later, He would explain to me why He had bent down on one knee. It happened while I was telling someone the precious story of my marriage proposal. The Lord said to me, "Remember, I got down on one knee for you, too." Knowingly and thankfully, I responded in my thoughts and from the heart, *Yes, Lord, I remember. You did do that for me, didn't You?*

Straightening His knee and standing up, Jesus told us that it was time to go. He began to rise in the air. A number of people in the group also began to ascend, but I was still just standing there. I began to feel very heavy, as if I weighed a thousand pounds. People all around me were rising, but I was firmly planted on the ground. I was about to cry out to Jesus for help when I, too, began to rise. I couldn't believe it; I was lifting off the ground! I pinched myself again; just like the first time, it hurt. As we all continued to rise, the air around us became cooler, the wind picked up, and the ground rapidly shrank beneath us.

We rose until we reached an altitude of five miles above the earth. I'm not sure how I knew this; I just did. There was a platform right in the middle of the air where Jesus positioned us all. He said He had to return to earth to take care of some things, and that He would return to us soon. We all settled back to wait. I sat on the side of the platform with my feet dangling over the edge and looked down, wondering what Jesus had gone to do. A few minutes later, Someone sat down next to me. I glanced over and realized that it was Jesus. I could see His feet and His clothes out of the corner of my eye.

I assumed that if these really were the end times, Jesus would not be next to me; He would be next to each person. I turned around to see if He was standing next to everyone else. Much to my surprise, He was not. As a matter of fact, they were all looking at me, and for some reason, I was able to hear their thoughts. In unison, they were asking, *Why is He with you?* I lifted my hands out to the side, palms facing up, shrugged my shoulders, and, with a questioning look, silently mouthed the words, *I don't know.*

Then I turned to Jesus, wanting to talk to Him, but I froze. What to say to the Son of God? I mean, seriously; He knows everything. He created me. I suddenly thought about bringing up the book of Deuteronomy. I figured doing that would make me look like a serious and well-read Christian. I didn't really know anything about Deuteronomy, but I hoped that Jesus would be impressed and would carry the conversation from there.

I began to lift my head, but I could not look directly at His face. I saw the fine hair on the backs of His hands; I saw His long, flowing dark hair, but I could not look Him in the eye. I knew that if I did, He would see right through me: right into my soul, right into my sin. I lifted my head enough to see His beard. It was not well-trimmed, unlike most men's beards today. I could see little hairs growing down toward His neck. I could tell that He was gazing at me; I just couldn't look at Him.

Once again, I tried to lift my head, but I couldn't. Instead, I said, "Lord, I...I...." and then lowered my head in shame. "I'm sorry," I finally whispered. I felt like a fake. I was sure I didn't love Him as much as the people standing behind me did, and I was also sure that, at any moment, Jesus was going to expose my hypocritical heart in front of all the others.

Suddenly, I felt His strong hands on both sides of my face. He lifted my head and looked right into my eyes. We were less than a foot apart. I tried to lower my head again, but He took His right hand and put it under my chin, forcing me to look directly at Him. I finally lifted my eyes, and as my gaze met His, wild love struck me once again. His look told me that no one controlled how deeply or how passionately He loved. His dark brown eyes were filled with warmth and affection. No face had ever looked so full of grace and love. I was undone.

Looking even more deeply into my eyes, He smiled and gently said, "Shhh." Then He said, "I love you. You need to know that. For what I have planned for you, you will need to know that." Next, He took my head and laid it upon His breast. He put His arms around me, held me close, and then started to rock me like a father would rock a young child. Suddenly, I began to cry—gently, at first; but, a short time later, I started weeping from deep within my soul. I realized at that moment that my own father had never held me like this.

With Jesus' arms around me, holding me tight, I felt safe and at home. As I continued to cry, Jesus leaned over and whispered softly in my ear, "I love you. It's all right. I'm here. You need to know how deeply I love you." I was filled with comfort as He continued to rock me, and then He lovingly kissed my head. Suddenly, a ball of fire shot out of His heart and into mine. It hit me as forcefully as if I'd been punched in the chest with a sledgehammer. I fell backward and found myself back in my apartment.

Seeing my bed, I went over to it and lay down. I was still crying deep, heavy sobs that wouldn't stop. After a while, I finally came to the end of my tears. I sat up and noticed that my pillow was so wet, it was dripping water when I lifted it. I then placed my hand on the area of my mattress that had been directly beneath my pillow, and as I pushed down, bubbles of water rose between my fingers. I had not only wept through my pillow; I had even soaked my mattress with my tears. How long had I been crying, and what had brought on all those tears?

A few days later, someone asked me a question about my father. Usually, when the subject of my father came up, I instantly felt an ache in the pit of my stomach. This time, however, I felt nothing negative. As a matter of fact, I felt great warmth toward my dad, even compassion. I felt no hurt or pain. I tried. I thought of events that had produced pain in the past, but there was nothing in me that hurt. Instead, I began to feel a sense of deep understanding and compassion for what he must have gone through while he was a prisoner of war.

It was then that I knew what had happened to me several days prior. Jesus had hugged and rocked the pain away as His wild love washed over and through me. Tears of healing had flowed from me, and now I felt like a different person.

7

KNOWING THE FATHER'S HEART

How was I supposed to begin? Though I could clearly hear my father talking about this year's crop, all that was going through my mind was, What do I say? Better yet, what will he say? Maybe this isn't a good idea. Yeah, there's probably a better time to do this than at a Fourth of July party with all the family around. What was I thinking? *Then I realized it wasn't my thinking that had brought me there. It was His—my Father's. And one thing I knew: He had only good for me.* All right, Papa, I thought. I trust You.

⌒

I didn't know of anyone who'd had an experience like mine. Carol had mentioned that her pastor had received a vision, but when I heard him describe it, I realized it was nothing like what I had gone through. I decided not to tell anybody about what had happened to me. I felt like the best way to protect the work God had done in me—the work He was still doing—was to avoid opening myself up to the possibility of someone suggesting that maybe I had just been exhausted and had taken a nap, or had eaten a bad piece of bologna, or that my pillow had been drenched by spilled water rather than my own tears.

Other people noticed a change in me, however, and a few vocalized their thoughts, asking me what was different. My brother took me by surprise when he said, "I don't know what's going on with you. You're still funny, but there's something more of a man about you. There's a settledness in you that didn't used to be there."

I told him, "I think I know what happened. I had a little face-to-face with Jesus recently."

"That must have been it," he said. "You don't turn everything into a joke anymore. I mean, I always knew there was depth in you, I just hadn't seen it much."

I smiled at his backhanded compliment. I love my brother.

He was right, however. For a while, I had been using humor to cover up what was really going on inside of me. But experiencing Jesus' wild love for me had melted away my insecurities and built my confidence to a level where I was able to start showing other people the real me. I was also looking forward to seeing who the real me was.

A bullet was shot into my fearful heart when I saw Jesus and experienced His wild love. I understood for the first time that Jesus' love for me was the same as the Father's love for me. Up until then, it had been hard for me to read Scriptures referring to God as Father. The Person of Jesus had always fascinated me, and the Holy Spirit had always seemed pretty mysterious (we Catholics referred to Him as the Holy Ghost), but I'd always assumed that God the Father wasn't crazy about me. I knew He loved me. But I just thought that, because He was God, He *had* to.

My view of God the Father had been significantly shaped by my relationships with my natural father and with other authority figures in my life, as happens to many people. But when I experienced Jesus' wild love for me, it changed my opinion of what God thought about me; and that, in turn, changed what I thought about myself, what I thought about God, and what I thought about other people. I learned firsthand that our view of God the Father will always be faulty if it is based on our success or failure in human relationships. Our view of the Father will also color our estimation of ourselves and of others. My own father had treated me judgmentally; as a result, I believed God the Father to be judgmental, and I felt I was continually being judged and found lacking. Living inside that mercy-less and grace-less mind-set caused me to judge myself and others harshly, too.

The assumption that I didn't measure up to God's standards had blinded me to the truth of God's love, even when it was right in front of me, in His written Word. Up until that time, I had merely skimmed over passages such as Ephesians 3:

> I pray that you, being rooted and established in love, may
> have power, together with all the Lord's holy people, to grasp
> how wide and long and high and deep is the love of Christ,

and to know this love that surpasses knowledge—that you
may be filled to the measure of all the fullness of God.
                                        (Ephesians 3:17–19 NIV)

But now, I was thrilled and elated at the prospect of a life of discovering how much God loves me, and of being *"filled to the measure of all the fullness of God."* Everywhere I turned in the Scriptures, in the Old Testament as well as in the New, I saw the ways in which He loved me. Where I had seen only judgment in the past, I now saw His love.

In the past, Jesus' face had been a blank. But now that I had looked deeply into His bright eyes and had been comforted by the tenderness of His smile, I felt that I was right there in the middle of every biblical account of His life. In the Word, whenever Jesus was said to have looked at someone, He was looking at me. The event may have happened over two thousand years ago, but it was as though I was right there, experiencing it firsthand. With just one gaze into my eyes, He had forever changed the way I would gaze into His.

How can all that occur in an instant? I am convinced that the heart is moved by what the eyes behold. It's in the beholding—the place of really seeing—that the heart is open to the movements of God. We see things, but we don't always *behold* things.

Let me explain. When I first saw the woman who would later be my wife, I didn't really *behold* her. It was early spring 1977, and I had recently moved to Schenectady, New York. A few friends invited me to play softball with them. When I arrived at the softball field, I noticed a young woman talking to a man I later learned was the pastor of a nearby church. She had dark hair that flowed past her waist, and she wore a big poncho that almost completely engulfed her. She spent the afternoon engrossed in conversation with the pastor, her thoughts clearly not on the game.

A group of us decided to go to a local pizza place after the game. I was to carpool with a friend but found myself in conversation with someone and ended up missing my ride. I'd assumed that the person I was talking with was going for pizza, too, but he needed to go straight home. I headed to the parking lot, hoping to find someone else from the group who hadn't left yet.

When I reached the parking lot, the poncho girl flagged me over, introduced herself as Laura, and asked if I could help start her car. It was a tiny 1977 Honda Civic, and she explained that her father had gone with her to buy it earlier that very day. She was not yet comfortable driving the standard-transmission car with its manual choke—a component she hadn't even known existed. I came over and showed her what the choke was and how it worked, started up the car, and asked her if she was going for pizza. When she said yes, I volunteered to drive us both over to the restaurant. We joined our friends and ended up having a very pleasant evening. After that, I saw Laura fairly regularly. I ended up going to the church she attended, and she started coming to a coffeehouse our group organized on Friday and Saturday nights.

There was nothing romantic going on between us; ours was just a nice friendship surrounded by a group of mutual friends. As time went by, my roommate, who had been spending quite a bit of time with Laura, mentioned that Laura might be interested in me. I laughed it off and said that since he spent so much time with Laura, he should just go out with her. He replied, more seriously, that she wasn't interested.

I liked Laura as a friend, but I wasn't really interested in her. I even remember once saying that she was an amazing person who would one day be a wonderful wife to someone. I went so far as to acknowledge that she was the kind of girl I'd want to marry someday—not her, specifically, just "that kind of girl," whatever that meant. As time passed, I became busy with other things and saw less and less of Laura. My roommate continued to carve out time to spend with her, however, and I heard she had taken a job nearby.

A couple of months later, I was at a friend's house for a party. It was an open house, with guests arriving and departing all evening long. I was standing near the entryway when a beautiful girl with dark shoulder-length hair walked in the front door. She was stunning.

I turned to my friend. "Who is that girl?" I asked.

"That's Laura," he told me.

"Laura who?"

He looked at me like I had just arrived from outer space. With a bit of an attitude, he said, "That's Laura Rocissano."

I looked at her as if for the first time. "She's beautiful."

My friend turned to me, looked me right in the eyes, and said, "Well, it's about time you saw what everyone else has always known. Yes, Laura is beautiful; and, for some strange reason, I think she likes you."

Ten months later, Laura and I were married.

I eventually found out that on the first day we met, Laura had stood in the parking lot next to her car, waiting for everyone else to pass by, before she asked me for help. I've always liked that part of the story best.

How is it possible to know a person, see her face, and fail to see her real beauty? How can two people look at the same scene, object, or person and see two completely different things? I'm not sure how, but I know I did. I saw Laura at least once a week for months, but I never noticed her true beauty until one fine day when my eyes were opened. That's the key—having eyes that don't just look at something or someone but go beyond looking to really see the beauty that's there.

The apostle Paul addresses this very subject in his letter to the church at Ephesus. The Ephesians were rich beyond measure in Jesus, yet they were beggars in their hearts. They were surrounded by the grace of God, yet they could not see it. Paul spends the first several chapters of Ephesians describing all that the believers possess in Christ—adoption, forgiveness, redemption, inheritance, grace, and so much more—and then, before he goes on, he prays that God would help them to truly see Him:

> [I] *do not cease to give thanks for you, making mention of you in my prayers: that the God of our Lord Jesus Christ, the Father of glory, may give to you the spirit of wisdom and revelation in the knowledge of Him, the eyes of your understanding being enlightened....* (Ephesians 1:16–18)

Paul is not praying just for more wisdom or revelation, though either of those would be a good thing. He is asking the Lord to specifically give the people wisdom as to who He is, as well as a revelation of His true nature.

Paul is saying that wisdom and revelation are given to the church, first and foremost, that believers might see Jesus in all His fullness—to behold Him for who He is. The apostle was aware that we have physical eyes to see what's before us, but we need another set of eyes—the "eyes of our understanding"—to truly take in what we observe. It takes a revelation *from* God to have a revelation *of* God.

I finally understood what was meant by the "eyes of my understanding" when I saw Laura at the party that night. I had seen her time and again, but I never really *saw* her. Everyone around me kept singing her praises, but, for some reason, the eyes of my understanding were blinded. In a single instant, though, that all changed. From the moment I truly *saw* her, I began to fully *love* her.

In the same way, just a glance of the real God changes everything. That's why the apostle Paul prayed what he did for the Ephesians. He understood that if God answers our prayer to see Him more clearly, then we will begin to love Him more deeply. True understanding and true love go hand in hand, in human relationships as well as in our relationship with God.

In chapter 3 of Ephesians, Paul goes even further. He "bows his knee" in prayer again (see Ephesians 3:14), asking that God would grant the Ephesians *"to be strengthened with might through His Spirit in the inner man"* (verse 16). There it is again: our *"inner man"* with "inner eyes"—the eyes of understanding— needs God's help to see the beauty that is ever before us.

The importance of seeing clearly was again emphasized to me during a different series of events. At a church function, I was introduced to a gentleman by some friends who had told me what an incredible man he was and who expressed their excitement that he and I were finally meeting. The gentleman seemed nice but came across as detached, and he also appeared to be in a hurry to go somewhere. I must admit, I was not extremely impressed with him. A short time later, I met a young man at a pickup basketball game. He was fun to be with, and he played well, too. We had a wonderful time and ended up going out for a bite to eat after the game. In the course of our conversation, I realized that he was the son of the man I had met at the church function.

In the son, I saw someone of incredible life. He radiated great joy and had a depth about him that was way beyond his years. These traits did not come to him out of the blue, of course.

Reflected in his eyes and echoed by his voice were the qualities of his father. When I asked him about his dad, he talked on and on with such love and reverence that I was overwhelmed. He also mentioned some distressing news that his dad had just heard, which would have been weighing heavily on him at the time we were introduced at the church function. Finally, it all made sense.

I learned a couple of valuable lessons that day. One of those was the ongoing lesson not to judge others quickly. But an even greater lesson was the revelation that I was able to see the father through the son. A light that had been switched on soon after my face-to-face encounter with Jesus became even brighter when I realized that I need the Son in order to know. I need the Son in order to see. I need to know and see the Son, here and now, so that I can more fully see the Father's smile and understand the affection He has for me.

Experiencing Jesus' wild love for me was the doorway to see, to know, and to experience the love of the Father. Whether I was spending intimate time with Him by reading the Bible or praying, or whether I was just living out my daily life, at every turn, the Holy Spirit was unveiling Jesus, and thereby unveiling the Father to me.

Jesus conveyed the same idea in an exchange with Philip.

"If you had known Me, you would have known My Father also; from now on you know Him, and have seen Him." Philip said to Him, "Lord, show us the Father, and it is enough for us." Jesus said to him, "Have I been so long with you, and yet you have not come to know Me, Philip? He who has seen Me has seen the Father; how can you say, 'Show us the Father'? Do you not believe that I am in the Father, and the Father is in Me? The words that I say to you I do not speak on My own initiative, but the Father abiding in Me does His

works. Believe Me that I am in the Father and the Father is
in Me; otherwise believe because of the works themselves."

(John 14:7–11 NASB)

"*If you had known Me, you would have known My Father also.*"
What a stunning statement. If we see Jesus, we see the Father.
Said differently, whatever we see of Jesus is what we see of the
Father. Whatever we understand about Jesus, we understand
about the Father. This was a huge revelation for me. To equate
my understanding and knowledge of Jesus to an understanding of
the Father was not easy for me. I easily got that both Jesus and
the Father are all-knowing, all-powerful, and eternal. But trusting
that my heavenly Father has the same heart, love, and emotions as
Jesus required an extension of my own emotions that took me far
beyond my comfort zone. I had always seen Jesus as the understanding One, full of grace and mercy for even the most vile of
sinners. He knew pain and was acquainted with sorrow and grief.
(See Isaiah 53:3.) And the Father…well, He was distant. He probably just put up with me for Jesus' sake.

Through the words of John 14:7–11 and similar passages,
Jesus extends an invitation to us all. It's as if He is saying, "Hey,
here I am. Do you see Me? If you do, look carefully. Gaze upon
Me, and you will see My Father. I love because He loves; I
heal because He heals; I speak because He speaks. When you
glimpse an aspect of My essence, you are glimpsing Father God,
as well.

Consider the following words of Jesus, which confirm this:

The Son can do nothing of Himself, unless it is something
He sees the Father doing; for whatever the Father does,
these things the Son also does in like manner.

(John 5:19 NASB)

*The word which you hear is not Mine, but the Father's who
sent Me.*   (John 14:24 NASB)

When I read Jesus' words, *"He who has seen Me has seen the
Father"* (John 14:9), I realized the implication: "When you see
Me expressing My love, you see the Father expressing His love."
In light of my own experience, this meant that Jesus' expressions
of His wild love for me were expressions of the Father's wild
love for me. But in order for me to view the Father in this way,
I needed the help of the Holy Spirit. Thankfully, Jesus made us
this promise:

> *But the Helper, the Holy Spirit, whom the Father will send
> in My name, He will teach you all things, and bring to your
> remembrance all things that I said to you.*   (John 14:26)

My face-to-face time with Jesus had ignited my yearning to
know and experience even more of the breadth, length, height,
and depth of His love for me. Because Jesus is the Door (see John
10:1–10)—and the Gate, the Window, and every other entry
point into each different dimension, or aspect, of the Father—
my growing relationship with Him brought me face-to-face
with the multifaceted layers of my false view of the Father that
had clouded my view of myself and of other people.

The writer of Hebrews describes Jesus as *"the radiance of
God's glory and the exact representation of his being"* (Hebrews
1:3 NIV). It's pretty clear that Jesus is *"the exact representation"* of
His Father. He has the exact same look; the exact same heart,
thoughts, desires, capacity to love; the exact same everything.
Everything that Jesus is, the Father is, too. Therefore, when you
look at Jesus, you're looking at the Father. It doesn't get any sim-
pler, or any more beautiful, than that.

8

THE JOURNEY OF FORGIVENESS

Okay, so how long do I stand here? *I wonder. My dad is talking and pointing at one plant after another, and I'm right beside him, appearing connected; yet my mind is wandering all over the universe. One minute, I'm going back over my past; the next minute, I'm crafting words for my immediate future.*

Come on, Chris. You can do this, *I tell myself.* Remember, you're not alone.

About a year prior to this garden encounter with my dad, when I was living in New York City, I had met a gentleman whose relationship with his own father was very similar to mine. He had suffered under his dad's abuse for many years, and yet, as I listened to him talk about the man, I could hear the love he had in his heart for him. I was amazed that what had once been a relationship of cold indifference had grown over time into a close bond of love and care between father and son. This simple yet compelling story of forgiveness penetrated my soul and made a profound impact.

This gentleman spoke of giving the "gift of forgiveness" to his dad every time he saw him. After many years of receiving this gift, his father slowly began to express love back to him, in small ways at first, but then more and more in larger and more touching ways.

God used this message to encourage me that the issues with my dad could, and hopefully would, one day be resolved. But He also made it clear that at some point, I would need to be the one to initiate the resolution by reaching out. God wanted me to *pursue* my own father.

The perfect follow-up scenario would have been for me to jump in my car that very day and get it all resolved right then and there. But I knew better. Trying to pattern my own journey after someone else's could produce damaging results. Only God knew when I would be ready to put my gift of forgiveness for my father on the altar and leave it there without any expectations of a return.

In my own secret desires, though, prying open that door on my own would have looked something like this: I would share with my dad all the horrible things he had done; my dad would cry crocodile tears and repent, loudly and humbly; he would then readily admit his own guilt (in great detail); and finally, he would vow before heaven and earth that he would never, ever hurt me again. It all reminded me of an old song called "The Impossible Dream." Like I said, I knew better.

After our year in New York City, moving back to Rochester in 1981 was taking a concrete step toward my dad. I had been carrying within me the knowledge that God wanted me to make a greater heart connection with him, and living in the same city would make it easier to spend time with him on a regular basis. What actually happened when we did get together...well, that was another question.

It was March of 1981—spring planting season, on a number of levels—when Laura and I moved with our daughter, Andrea, to Rochester. Dad began having us over for the occasional lunch or dinner, and whenever we arrived, he was usually either in the middle of gardening or watching a TV program about gardening. Each visit turned into a mini-tour of what he'd planted that week and how all the other vegetables he'd put in earlier that season were doing.

Each time he offered these new seeds into the soil of our relationship, I accepted them wholeheartedly, being very purposeful about showing my interest in what he clearly considered to be important. Our visits often started in the garage, where he would show me the latest seed packets or plants he'd purchased. I would ask him a lot of questions and offer positive feedback to let him know that I valued the work he was doing and appreciated his sharing this part of his life with me. The tour would continue as we strolled around back so he could show me the garden's progress. In these moments, I worked on sowing seeds of my own into the relationship by telling him about the latest events in my life, in an effort to nudge him and his new wife, Marian, a little closer to my family.

Between his love for his wife and his love of gardening—a lifelong passion that seemed to intensify with his second marriage—Dad seemed to have found a new level of peace. It was as if the "garden" of his life had been leveled out, in much the same way as a gardener digs up fallow ground, adds a bit more dirt, and then smooths it out before planting new seeds. God had been removing debris, rocks, stones, and dead things out of the ground of Dad's heart while he was getting counseling and just living life. I could see that having someone to love, and being loved himself, had brought my father a new softness and sense of settledness. In addition, to honor Dad's tireless work on behalf of fellow veterans, our local congressman named Dad the top Veterans Affairs advocate in the district.

I should have been celebrating this and other successes with him. Instead, I was distracted by Marian's kids, who would remark from time to time on how harsh Dad was. Apparently, it was still the case that the man so beloved by outsiders struggled to earn that same love at home. At this point, a lot of "debris" in my father's life was blocking my ability to see the work that God was doing in him, so I remained focused on the tidbits of feedback that seemed to confirm my own negative opinions of him.

I should have been cheering for my father. And I was trying to, at least in the areas of his gardening and his new marriage. But I could not look at him without seeing a cruel man somewhere in the background, just waiting to emerge. I was beginning to celebrate the place he had reached; but the man he had been, and the man he was becoming—those parts were still being worked out.

Our relationship between 1981 and 1982 was a mixed bag. On one hand, I knew in my heart that there would be some form of reconciliation between us. On the other, in spite of my face-to-face encounter with Jesus when I experienced His love firsthand, I still found myself trapped behind a wall of intimidation. I had compassion for my father and a heartfelt desire to see things change, but, when push came to shove, I kept reverting to the little kid who was more afraid of his father than he was confident in love. It would take one more step for me to reach a point of being ready to reconcile.

During April of 1982, our second daughter, Katie, was born. She was a pistol right from the start; even when Katie was a newborn, Laura and I could tell that we had a strong, fearless little girl on our hands. Sure enough, as she grew, she exerted her independence and was never afraid to express what she was thinking.

As we first brought her home from the hospital and tended to her, something new struck my heart. Parenting was nothing new to us, but having two children suddenly made my role as a father vastly different. With only one child, a father can often play a limited role. With two or more, however, there's a constant need for a father to be engaged with his kids.

That got me thinking: now that my siblings and I were older, did our father ever feel a sense of loss when he thought of the years we lived apart from him? I guess I'd never thought about it before. I'd just assumed that Dad liked things the way they were. But then I realized that, although he was working through his own personal hell, he was home, and he was at least somewhat engaged with his three kids, no matter how warped our relationship may have been.

Considering all that, I became convinced that he must have felt loss for the years of separation. I knew he felt great love for his new wife, Marian, and that he and his brothers were still inseparable. If he could love them, he must have loved us; he just didn't know how to express that love in the midst of his pain. Home had been his prison. He had been responsible for everything, and yet everything seeped through his hands like water. But I wondered if, now that we were grown and no longer his responsibility, he could finally embrace us, as he'd perhaps always wanted to.

That was my question, and the only way I would get the answer was to step up to the plate and swing. The "plate" was the edge of the garden, and all I had to "swing" by way of a bat was the gift of forgiveness.

The gift of forgiveness. What a wonderful concept. Forgiveness is a lifelong lesson. For me, the learning really began at the age of twelve, when my dad took my brother, Mark, and me to Montreal to attend the 1967 World's Fair. It was one of many times we ventured into Canada with my father during our annual two-week summer vacation.

We stayed with some relatives who lived in a nice downtown apartment, and headed out early in the morning so that we could enjoy a full day at the fair. On our way through the lobby of the apartment complex, we came upon a man doing some tile work. My father greeted him with "Good day" as we passed. Wanting to say the right thing, I also said, "Good day" and smiled, as my father had. When we got outside, my father turned around and slapped me hard across the face. He struck me with such force that I started to fall backward, but my brother caught me.

Other pedestrians on the crowded sidewalk stopped to stare, and then slowly walked on. I was stunned. I looked at my father and saw that he was fuming. Pressing my hand to my face, I asked him, "What was that for?"

"Because of your sarcastic and mocking comment to that man back there," he replied, then turned and started walking.

I had no idea what he meant. I wanted to cry, but I wasn't about to give my father the satisfaction of seeing me tear up.

Standing next to me, my brother asked, "Are you okay?" Then he said, "I think Dad felt you were mocking him and the man working back there by repeating exactly what he said." I was telling my brother that I wasn't trying to mock anyone when we heard our father say, "Come on, boys. We don't have all day."

Actually, we did have all day. All week, too. But I didn't want to spend even the next minute with him.

I was mad, and I intended to hold on to my anger as long as I could. It would be my "special gift" to my dad. The gift of unforgiveness.

As we drove to the fair, my father acted as if nothing had happened, which only made things worse. We parked and joined the throngs of happy people. I was part of the throng, but I wasn't happy.

Like a child who runs away from home, only to return later in the day when he gets hungry (I actually did that when I was five), it's hard to stay angry when you're at the World's Fair, especially at the age of twelve. There were games, rides, attractions, and every kind of junk food imaginable. I was in heaven. The only problem was, I couldn't bear to let my dad know I was having a good time. I had to cloak my joy with a sullen attitude and angry face. Oh, I was still angry; I just couldn't enjoy my anger as much as I would have liked.

We'd been at the fair a few hours when my father leaned over to me and said, "Mark told me you weren't trying to mock me. I'm sorry I hit you."

I couldn't look him in the eye, so I just nodded and grunted, "Okay." It took me a while to let go, but I eventually found myself smiling and truly enjoying the day. I also realized that my dad was trying, at least, which gave me an unfamiliar sense of compassion toward him as I allowed myself to let go of my anger and forgive him in my heart, at least as much as I knew how to do. After that, the slapping event was largely forgotten and mostly forgiven. Total forgiveness would come later.

Another lesson in forgiveness happened the summer before my senior year of high school. I saw a girl at our county fair (I know—sounds like trouble already, right?). She had been going out with a guy I had met just once, but she told me they had recently broken up. We had a nice conversation and then spent the evening walking around the fairgrounds, taking in the sights. It was all very innocent, and we never saw each other again after that night. But a couple of weeks later, her ex-boyfriend and four other guys jumped me from behind in a parking lot. Five on one was not a fair fight, and I ended up bruised, bloodied, and unconscious. A friend pulled me into his car and drove me home.

In the wake of that fight, I battled a combination of hatred and fear in my heart. The ex-boyfriend lived in a nearby town, so I never knew when I might come upon him in my frequent travels for sports. I was always looking over my shoulder for any suspicious movement. I had no desire to forgive the guy. It didn't even occur to me. I felt far too empowered by my anger and hatred.

It turned out that the guy wasn't done with me, after all. In March of my senior year, he was dating the same girl again, and he couldn't bear the thought that someone else had "claimed" his girlfriend's heart, even for just one evening. After a night of heavy drinking, he pulled together three carloads of guys and headed for my house.

My best friend, Tom, called to warn me. Good thing, because I was on my way to answer a knock at the door when he called. I picked up the phone, and the first thing Tom said was, "If someone knocks on your door, don't answer it!" I leaned over and locked it, instead. Tom quickly told me that they had been to his house, looking for me, and Tom's father chased them away with a shotgun. Another knock sounded, and I ignored it.

I wondered how the group had found out where I lived, and Tom explained that another kid from our high-school class was with them and had offered to guide them to my house. Well, he'd made good on his offer. I looked out the side window and saw three cars parked down the street. Then I saw the guys outside. One of them was holding a tire iron, and another one held some chains. It was like being in a bad movie.

Feeling unsafe in my own house, I jumped out a back window and headed across town to my cousin's place. From there, I called the cops, who went to my house and ordered the kids to leave. They followed up with a restraining order against each of the guys from the other town. The only kid who slipped through the cracks was the guy from my high school. I decided to deal with him myself.

The following week, I confronted the kid at his locker. He turned around, and there I was. I grabbed him by the shirt collar, picked him up, and slammed him against the locker. After the second slam, a teacher grabbed us both and pulled us into his empty classroom. "What's this all about?" he asked me, and so I told him. Then he turned to the other kid. "Is this true?" he asked. The kid nodded his head yes. The teacher then said, "Let's go down to the gym right now and get you some gloves. I'll watch over the fight myself." (Things sure were different then.) The teacher and I stood up to go, but the other kid just sat there. With a sheepish expression, he dropped his head and said, with halting speech, "No need. I screwed up." Then he looked at me. "I'm really sorry, Chris."

Now what? I thought. I wasn't a believer at the time, and I had only a cursory understanding of forgiveness. I knew one thing, though: I had to look tough. But when I looked over at the kid and saw the pathetic expression on his face, I found myself instantly filled with compassion for him. *What's happening to me?* I wondered. *Am I really going to forgive him? No, I can't do that. Please, somebody stop me. No, no...yes. Yes, I can. And*

I did. Though we never became close—graduation was just a couple of months away, after all—we did become closer. That's what forgiveness does: it builds bridges. Reconciliation will not always happen. Jesus didn't say, "Reconcile." He said, "Forgive." (See, for example, Mark 11:26.)

Forgiveness is a universal necessity in every aspect of God's creation, and not only among humankind. A recent study of primates suggests that forgiveness is an important part of their health. Observing a group of primates, their handlers noticed that when one larger primate harmed two smaller ones within the group, both smaller primates separated from the group and spent some time alone. Soon, one of the smaller primates returned to the group and interacted with the larger animal that had harmed it. When this occurred, the smaller primate was quickly received by the group. The other smaller primate remained distant; even when approached by some of the other primates, it would not interact with them. It wasn't long before this particular primate became very sick with a stomach ailment. Shortly thereafter, it fell gravely ill and died. The other primate that returned to the group lived a long and happy life. It seems even monkeys know that forgiveness is a wise way to live.

Although the lessons in forgiveness that I learned along the way were never easy, they were all necessary steps that brought me to the place of being prepared to extend the gift of forgiveness to my father. Unlike the time in Montreal when I accepted my dad's apology mostly because it enabled me to move on and enjoy myself at the fair, I knew that this would be an all-encompassing expression of total forgiveness, without any expectation of apology or reconciliation on his part.

The gift of forgiveness. It was time to apply the lessons I'd learned.

9

THE GIFT OF FORGIVENESS

Okay, Lord. Here we go.

I interrupted my father mid-sentence and said, "Hey, Dad. Can I talk to you a minute?"

He stopped what he was saying and simply said, "Sure. What's up?"

I had planned and practiced a very articulate little speech, but I completely lost track of it and instead blurted out, "You know everything that happened to me—to us—when I was young?" I had hoped he would know what I was talking about so I wouldn't have to say more.

He hesitated a moment, then quietly responded, "Yeah."

I'm sure he thought I was about to dredge up the past and throw it in his face. But I wasn't. I remembered my little speech, and I knew it wasn't the right thing to say. That little speech went out the window.

He was still facing the garden, now with a blank look on his face. I couldn't read him, but I knew I wasn't supposed to. I was just to forgive him. That's the gift. So I said, "I just want you to know that I love you and I forgive you for everything that ever happened."

I expected him to either erupt or walk away. He did neither. Instead, he remained standing there, quietly. That was even worse. He didn't say a word; he didn't move a muscle. I wasn't sure what to do, so I just waited. As I was standing there, I heard a still, small voice say, "Put your arm around him." I wanted to rebuke the voice, but I knew who it was. I said inside, *No, Lord. Please don't make me do that. Let me wait to see what he's going to do.* Again, I heard, "Put your arm around him." This time, I obeyed. I extended my right arm and put it around my father's shoulders. I had no idea what to expect.

The moment my hand came to rest on his right shoulder, he began to weep. It began as a soft, gentle cry; but as I held him, it deepened until his whole body was trembling. Suddenly, he raised his left hand and put it around my waist. I was immediately filled with compassion and love for him, and I, too, began to cry.

In the middle of a Fourth of July picnic, with everyone else standing thirty feet behind us, there stood my dad and I, holding onto each other and weeping like babies. We stayed just like that for another minute, crying and literally holding each other up. After a few more moments, we both began to settle down. Still, neither of us said a word.

As we stood there, dripping wet, I realized that we had nothing to use to dry our tears. With my free hand, I wiped my eyes; then, with my hand full of tears, I pointed to the garden and said, "Look at how high that corn is." My dad laughed, knowing I was trying to cover up our act of drying our eyes before we turned around to face the rest of the family. He followed suit, swiping his hand over his cheeks before pointing in the same direction and saying, "Well, take a look at how big that lettuce is getting." It was my turn to chuckle. For the next several moments, we went back and forth, wiping our faces clean and making funny comments about the garden.

When we finally felt cleaned up enough, we turned around, gave each other another quick hug, and headed back to join the rest of the family. I wasn't sure if anyone had seen the exchange between my father and me. As a matter of fact, my father and I never talked about that moment again. It was a special time, captured forever in our hearts—the hearts of the two people who needed it most.

Laura and I on our wedding day, April 29, 1978. And yes—I did marry up!

My lovely daughters when they were young,
with me and my Tom Selleck mustache.

One of my dad's favorite places: the classroom. He was the consummate teacher.

My dad and his brothers at their favorite place—the St. Lawrence River. Thumbs-up, Dad!

PART THREE:
A FATHER'S WILD LOVE

10

PAPA'S KISS

For years, I had been distant and cold toward my father. Now, suddenly, we were not just relating to each other; we were actually enjoying our relationship. We regarded each other with new eyes. I now saw him as a man who had gone through a horrible experience and needed his son's acceptance, and he now saw me as a son who had been hurt and needed to know his father's love. It was finally a perfect fit.

At the church where my family attended at the time, everyone was so close that the act of hugging was as common as a handshake. One sunny Sunday afternoon shortly after that memorable exchange beside the garden, our family went directly from church to my father's house for lunch. He opened the door to welcome us, and as we filed inside, I reached out without thinking and gave him a big bear hug. My father and I had hugged before, but never like that. He looked at me, and I could tell that although the hug had caught him off guard, he'd enjoyed it.

When the visit was over and it was time to go, my family and I headed for the door. My father was standing there with arms extended, waiting for another bear hug. I went over and put my arms around him. We held each other a bit longer this time. Already, a new love and a new trust between us were beginning to grow.

From that day forward, whenever my father and I would greet each other, we embraced with great warmth. Thus began a decade of slow yet deliberate growth in mutual trust and affection. Every time our family would arrive at his home, his arms would be opened wide to receive us.

My kids loved his greetings. Even now, one of their fondest memories is their grandpa leaning down to give them a kiss. He would sometimes rub his unshaven cheeks against their soft skin, making them squeal and giggle.

Something changed in me when I watched my father interact with my children. His tenderness toward them showed me what was really inside. When he embraced them, I was able to receive the gesture for myself. He could still be a little surly from time to time (just ask his stepchildren), but he was making great strides toward wholeness and kindness.

In the course of time, I was invited back to a Catholic community in a beautiful rural area outside Albany, New York, that I had visited in the seventies. When I arrived, the gentleman at the door greeted me, not with a handshake or even a hug, but a kiss upon the cheek.

The kiss threw me for a moment, and the man noticed my awkward look. He looked at me and said, "Sorry if I just made you uncomfortable, but we believe in the importance of an honorable greeting. As it says in Romans 16:16, '*Greet one another with a holy kiss.*'"

For the next few days, I was inundated with kisses on the cheek. It was uncomfortable at first, but I quickly got used to it. By the end of the week, not only did I feel completely at ease with the situation, but I was becoming a kisser. I was probably kissing dogs and trees when the time came to head home.

I drove back on a Saturday. After church on Sunday, our family took off for my father's house. Upon our arrival, I fell into his arms. But instead of giving him just a hug, without even thinking, I planted a big kiss on his right cheek.

I couldn't believe it. I had just kissed my father.

He stepped back and stared at me. I didn't think he was angry, but I wasn't sure what he was thinking. Suddenly, he smiled and said, "I like that." Then he stepped up to me and planted a big kiss on my right cheek. "Yep, I like that," he said again.

There was always a father's kiss to say hello or good-bye. Every kiss seemed to wash my soul, giving me greater affection for my dad and also releasing even greater affection for my own children. I was beginning to realize how deeply true affection empowers the heart. We love because we're loved. "*We love because* [God] *first loved us*" (1 John 4:19 NIV).

For the first time in my life, I began to look forward to time with my dad. It was a wonderful feeling.

Apparently, he felt the same way about seeing me. I can remember coming down his street one day, and noticing that the drapes over the front window were pulled back. As we came closer to the house, I saw the drapes fall. When we pulled into the driveway, my father came out the front door and made a bee-line for the car. Even before I'd turned off the engine, Dad had opened my door and was pulling me out of the car. He hugged me, kissed me on the cheek, and then escorted us to the house.

Once we'd gone in, Marian pulled me aside. "Your dad has been at the window for almost an hour," she told me. "When I asked him why he was standing there, he said, 'I can't wait to see Chris.'"

She told me that she'd asked him why, and he'd replied with a smile, "I just want to kiss his face."

I just want to kiss his face. I loved those words.

Life continued with a lightness to our relationship that carried us through the years. The moments that tested this new season were few and far between.

Almost ten years after our moment in the garden, my father called and asked if I could come over. I jumped in the car and drove straight to his place. When he opened the door, there was a soberness to him that I hadn't seen in a long time. He led me into the living room and asked me to sit down. Then he pulled out a large sleeve that I knew contained X-rays. He handed it to me and asked me to take them out.

I slid the first X-ray out and held it up to the light. Having spent years working as a surgical technician, I had seen hundreds of X-rays. But I had never seen an X-ray that looked like this. It was a chest X-ray, but instead of showing a localized area where there might be a tumor or some other specific issue, the entire X-ray looked like it was encased in fog. The whole thing was just a big gray area. You could make out the lungs, but it was like looking through a cloudy filter.

My father said that the doctor told him he didn't know what was going on, and he would need to come to the hospital for a lung sample—a simple outpatient procedure under local anesthesia. The next moment, I heard a still, small voice inside me say, "Go with your father whenever he has to go to the doctor or to the hospital." *Okay*, I thought. I had my marching orders.

I went along for my dad's follow-up appointment and confirmed that no one was quite sure what was going on. Dad's doctor hemmed and hawed; he would not commit to any specific diagnosis, though he finally discussed the possibility that it was cancer. When we asked for a prognosis, he gave only a vague answer, saying that he really didn't know what was ailing my father. He scheduled the outpatient procedure for the following day.

Early the next morning, I went to pick up my father. As we drove to the hospital, I could tell he was nervous. He asked what the procedure was like, and after I had told him, he said, "Sorry I asked."

"Don't be nervous, Dad. It will be over very quickly," I assured him.

He told me he wasn't nervous about the procedure; he was nervous about what they would find. We prayed together as we pulled into the hospital parking lot. It was so nice to be connected to my father's heart.

After we located the outpatient surgical area, Dad got all dressed in his best hospital garb. No-nonsense guy that he is, he walked out of the bathroom as if he owned the place and headed straight for me. He looked a little too "breezy," so I had him turn around. Sure enough, he was two cheeks to the wind, giving a free show to everyone else in the waiting room. I tied his gown shut in the back, and then we sat down to wait until his name was called.

When my father was summoned, we both stood up. I asked to be seated near his head during the procedure. The surgeons granted my request because they knew me from work.

The procedure began normally, but I soon realized that they were having trouble getting a specimen from my father's lung. Each attempt meant more needle pricks, more trocar invasions, and more pain for my dad. Finally, after what seemed like forever, they gave up. "That's enough trauma for one day, Mr. DuPré," the doctor said. "I'm sorry we could not get what we needed. It doesn't appear we will, if we continue to go through this way. We'll have to reschedule you to return and use another entry point."

My dad whispered to me, "Wow. Now, that's some great news." I started laughing, as did the doctor, who'd overheard. After my dad had changed back into his clothes, we scheduled an appointment for the following week and then left the hospital.

When I picked up my dad for the second attempt at the procedure, he looked a bit more nervous than the previous time. Knowing what he had experienced the week before, I couldn't blame him. I tried to reassure him that it would go better, but he told me for the second time that the procedure was not what he was nervous about.

He then confessed to me that his greatest fear was a diagnosis of lung cancer, and of suffocating, slowly and painfully, as it metastasized. His words made me aware of a longtime phobia I'd never noticed before. My dad had always worn his dress shirts too large so the collars would not press against his neck, especially when he was wearing a tie. Whenever he went for a haircut, he would come home covered in hair because he never allowed the barber to fasten the cape very tightly around his neck. I'd been aware of these things, but suddenly, it all made sense: Dad hated the feeling of being choked, and death by suffocation would be the worst possible way for him to go. We prayed then and there that his greatest fear would never come to pass.

The second hospital visit went much like the first. The surgeons tried another entry point, with more needle pricks, more trocars invading Dad's body, and more pain. In the end, the result was the same: No specimen. I had a funny feeling I knew what they would say next, and it ended up that I was right. The doctor said that the only remaining method available to get a specimen was a lung biopsy. In this fairly simple procedure, the surgeon makes a small incision in the chest, cuts through to the ribcage, separates two ribs, and inserts a long, thin instrument to extract a small specimen of the lung. The only reason they hadn't attempted this method yet was that a lung biopsy required general anesthesia instead of merely local anesthesia.

The doctor gave my father about a week to heal after the second attempt under local anesthesia and then went ahead and scheduled him for a lung biopsy.

On the appointed day, Marian took Dad to the hospital, and I met them there. When I entered his room, I found him sitting on the edge of his bed. His shirt was off, and I was alarmed to see the red blotches covering his upper body. I hid my concern and went right to him for a hug.

I was permitted to wheel him down to the surgical holding room, with Marian following. We entered the holding room and met the nurse on duty, whose job it was to make sure she had the right patient going in for the right procedure. Everything checked out, and we found a spot to park the stretcher.

About fifteen minutes later, another nurse entered the holding area and called Dad's name. Dad lifted his hand, and she came over. She was the circulating nurse, charged with keeping things running smoothly in the surgical room. She went through the same steps that the holding-room nurse had gone through earlier. Very thorough and very professional.

As she was finishing, a horde of masked men in green scrubs came through the door. Leading the charge was the attending surgeon—the doctor who would perform the surgery. He was followed by a surgical resident, an anesthesiologist, and a third-year medical student. It was a veritable wall of green.

The attending surgeon—an excellent doctor I had worked with many times over the years—introduced everyone on the team to Marian and me, then told my father that it was time to say good-bye to us. Marian leaned over and gave him a kiss. I was too embarrassed to kiss him in front of so many people, so I lowered my right hand into the stretcher and gave him a "cool guy" handshake.

My father looked at me like I was nuts. He said, "Oh, no. That won't do." He then proceeded to yank on my hand, dragging my body over the edge of the stretcher. By the time he stopped pulling, I was almost fully in the stretcher, with the tips of my toes just barely touching the floor. The team of doctors had started to move, but they stopped to see what would happen next.

My dad took my face in both his hands. He looked at me, then pulled my face toward him and kissed me on both cheeks. I quickly lost my "cool" and allowed myself to enjoy the moment. Then Dad turned my head so that I was facing the surgical team. Dad looked right at the team and said, with great pride and love, "This is my son. I love him."

I was stunned. It was obvious the surgical team was, too. They nodded awkwardly, looked at one another, and began to head out.

My dad turned back to me and said, "Nope, that's not good enough."

Clearly unsure of what that meant, the surgical team stopped and turned around again.

My father mouthed the words "I love you" to me before pulling my face toward his once again and kissing me. I will never forget this moment: my father, totally unashamed of me, his son, lavishing me with kisses. He released me, then turned to the nurse. "Okay," he said. "Now I'm ready."

The nurse started wheeling him toward the elevators, which were about thirty feet away. But before they'd gone even ten feet, my father yelled, "Stop!" The nurse halted the stretcher right away, and the entire surgical team stopped in their tracks yet again.

"What's wrong, Mr. DuPré?" the nurse asked.

"I can't see my son when you wheel me in this direction," my father replied. "Please turn me around."

The nurse smiled at me; I grinned back as my eyes filled with tears.

She rotated the stretcher so that my father was facing me and Marian and began pulling him toward the elevators. I blew Dad a kiss, and he blew one back to me. Then he started a series of kisses that had everyone laughing. He blew a kiss, pretended to load a gun, and "shot" me with kisses; then he kissed his finger and flicked it to me before simply blowing me more kisses. And in between kisses, he was signing "I love you" with his hands. The surgical team were just incredulous. I must admit, it was fun to observe their reactions.

Finally, the nurse pulling the stretcher arrived at the elevator. The doors opened, and the nurse wheeled Dad inside. As the door began to close, he shifted in his stretcher, leaned over the left side, and blew me one last kiss, ending with his thumb of approval raised high in the air and with a big smile on his face. Then the door closed, and he was on his way.

The members of the surgical team looked at me and smiled awkwardly before turning and walking off. The holding-room nurse came over to me and said, "I have never seen anything like that before. I love to see a father who loves his children."

Struggling to hold back my tears, I managed to respond with a quiet "Me too."

Marian and I headed for the lounge outside the surgical wing to wait during the hour-long procedure. I grabbed a newspaper and sat down, but I found it hard to concentrate on the pages in front of me. I was still enjoying the high that came from my father's blatant show of affection for me. Sitting there in the lounge gave me time to drink it all in. It also gave me time to think.

I had recently been reading through Luke 15, which records a series of Jesus' parables that includes the story of the prodigal son. As I studied this parable in detail, I came to realize that the prodigal son was just one character among many, and that the story is really about the father. The younger son goes broke, having wasted his precious inheritance. Not knowing how his father will react, he heads home anyway, hoping against hope that he will be permitted to return, even if it's as a servant. At least that way, he'd get something to eat.

As the prodigal son shuffles up the road, his father sees him from afar. When I read this part, my thoughts drifted to my own dad, standing at the front window with the curtain pulled aside, waiting for me to arrive so that he could run out and give me a kiss. "I just want to kiss his face," he told his wife.

The father in Luke 15 was waiting, too. He was waiting to lavish his son with kisses and love—not a love dependent upon the son's obedience but a love based upon the father's own goodness. There's a huge difference.

The moment the father sees his son coming, he takes off in his direction, eager to greet him. I have this feeling that when the son saw his father, he became very nervous. The culture of that day permitted women, children, and slaves to run; but it was shameful for men to run unless they were going into battle. Was this father going into battle? Against his son? Whatever the son thought, he decided to stay put and not flee. He would live or die in his father's presence.

As the father got closer, the son must have seen his smile. He must have seen the joy on his father's face, dispelling any thoughts of battle. When his father reached his son, he immediately "*fell on his neck and kissed him*" (Luke 15:20). The word used here for "*kissed*" is actually a present progressive verb that means "to kiss and kiss and keep on kissing." As the son was kissed over and over, the shame in his soul was lifted away and removed.

I believed I knew just how that son must have felt. I had just been kissed by my own father over and over, and I had seen unmistakable joy on my father's face. Sitting there during the surgery gave me time to pray and to bask in the love that my father had just lavished upon me.

Marian and I had sat in the lounge for a little over an hour when our names were called, and we were summoned to a small conference room. As we waited for the doctor, Marian asked me what would happen if they'd found out my dad had cancer. She and I hadn't specifically discussed that possibility until now, and she began to share how hard it would be to know she had only a year or two left with my dad.

We talked for a few minutes. I tried to encourage her, but my comments didn't seem to bring her much peace. In the middle of an emotional moment, the doctor very stoically walked in, followed by the anesthesiologist. I did not take this as a good sign.

The two men introduced themselves again, and all four of us sat down. I was eager to hear what they had found. Was Dad okay, or did he have cancer? If he did, what was his prognosis?

The attending surgeon looked back and forth between me and Marian several times, then finally settled his gaze on the space between us and said, "I'm sorry to have to tell you this, but Mr. DuPré passed away on the table shortly after we got started. We did all we could to revive him, but it was of no use. Again, I'm so sorry."

Marian let out a bloodcurdling scream and collapsed into my lap, weeping uncontrollably. I put my arms around her and held her tightly as I fought off my own tears. The two doctors sat there in silence, letting us absorb the news. After a short time, I asked the attending surgeon what had happened. He said they believed there was a blood clot trapped between the heart and the lungs, known as a pulmonary embolism.

Then I turned to the anesthesiologist. "I noticed how blotchy my father was this morning," I told him. "Did he get enough fluids before surgery?"

He looked at me like I had shot him in the chest. He hesitated for a moment, then said, "That's a question I've been asking myself. I believe he did. I feel we did everything we could do."

I appreciated his honesty. The attending surgeon then said, "We could order an autopsy, if you'd like, to determine the exact cause of death. But I think you need to know one thing. When we opened Mr. DuPré's chest cavity, we found no specific tumor. Instead, the entire chest cavity was filled with cancer. It covered every area. To be honest with you, I don't understand how he's been alive for so long."

Marian began to lift herself up. "I don't want an autopsy," she said. "He's been cut up enough."

I then asked the doctor, "If my father had lived through this surgery, what would have happened to him? What would have been his prognosis?"

He looked at me with eyes of steel. "He would have died within the next few months. Basically, it would have choked him from within. To be brutally honest with you, it would have been a horrible way to die."

In that moment, I realized that my father's death, though it was one of the most painful events of my life, had been a gift for him. Instead of experiencing his greatest fear—choking to death—he quietly went to sleep and woke up face-to-face with Jesus. Instead of suffering through a horribly painful, dragged-out death, he lavished love upon his family and then quietly and peacefully slipped into eternity.

I also realized the precious gift I had received that day. Instead of just a quick good-bye, as I would have given my father, he gave me the gift of extravagant affection. Embedded in my mind is my final memory of him: a father declaring his love for me, not out of duty but out of desire.

It became a living example for me of the face-to-face encounter I'd had with Jesus years earlier. For the second time in my life, I saw the face of love—wild love. A love that was not under the control of man. A love that was unashamed and full of passion. That day, my father gave me a gift for which I will be forever grateful. Thank you, Papa. I look forward to seeing you again, face-to-face.

The usual events followed. We met with a local funeral home and scheduled two consecutive days of viewings. The funeral director questioned our request for two full days, but we reassured him that both would be necessary. Then we headed back to Marian's house to gather as a family. My job was to phone a list of relatives. I placed some calls, each one bringing the pain of Dad's death back to life.

As I was getting ready to make another call, the phone rang. I picked it up and said, "Hello?"

"Oh, thank God, Dave," said a male voice. "I heard that you had died. It's so good to hear your voice."

For a moment, I couldn't speak.

"Hello, Dave?" the man said. "Are you there?"

"I'm so sorry," I finally replied, "but this is his son Chris. I hate to have to tell you this, but my father did pass away this morning."

I don't recall anything more from that conversation. I do remember that, after talking to that man, I sat there in a daze for quite a while. From then on, every time I answered the phone, I identified myself by name.

The wake went well—as well as a wake can go. The funeral director said that he couldn't remember the last time so many people had shown up at his funeral home. Partway through the second night, he said that we should have booked three days instead of two. We all laughed.

The local congresswoman came, as did many of the city's dignitaries. Because of my dad's involvement with the Veterans Administration, he had become a local hero to the area vets. They showed up in droves, as did many of his former students.

Over and over again, I heard, "Your dad was my favorite teacher." The joy for me was that I no longer responded negatively in my heart to these comments. I was able to rejoice with his former students and to celebrate the man who was my father. It was an emotional two days, but also a very warm and memorable two days.

The day after the wake, we had a funeral service at the church, followed by the burial at a local cemetery. Because Dad was a veteran, he was given a military service, complete with a twenty-one-gun salute. It was very moving for everyone present, and we left feeling saddened at the loss but also able to more clearly see the greatness of the man. He wasn't perfect, by any means; but with his passing, the fruit of his life came out from the shadows, and everyone got to see the impact he'd made on thousands of lives. Somehow I felt that I was near the top of that list.

11

THE GIFT KEEPS GIVING

On that day in June 1991, my father went in for surgery, was gently put to sleep, and never awakened again to this world. He entered another one, now face-to-face with Jesus.

Less than a year after my father's death, my mother began to feel ill. This was really nothing new, as she had endured one physical battle after another over the years. When I was little, I remember her making frequent visits to the doctor. The series of operations she underwent during the course of my childhood basically served as an introduction to human anatomy. What's a thyroid? It needs to come out. Where's your gall bladder? That goes, too. You say you quickly run out of breath? Your heart is bad. We'll leave it in there but give you some medication for it.

My mother kept a shelf of pills that would have put any pharmacy to shame.

Was my mother a hypochondriac? I don't know. As a child, that's not a question you ask or even a word you know. You may suspect it, but you'd never talk about it. What I do know is that, this time, when my mother described her pain, something seemed different. She went to the emergency room. When I arrived at the hospital, the doctor said that she was experiencing some kind of bowel discomfort. He thought she might be battling diverticulitis.

My mother was admitted, and the doctors began to administer treatment. Soon after, they prescribed some new medications and released her. Rather than returning to her apartment, where she would be alone, my mother went to stay at my brother's house. This was a painful period for her, and it wasn't long before she was back in the hospital. It turned out that the disease wasn't diverticulitis after all, but a horribly aggressive case of Crohn's disease.

Because she had been treated for other problems while the Crohn's disease had gone undetected, the disease had spread like wildfire. The doctors performed a temporary colostomy and flooded her body with new medications. When I went to see her, she was stable. She told me not to worry; she would be fine.

Around that time, I received a call from a friend in Kansas City who was looking for someone to teach seventh grade. I had taught junior high for four years, so I flew out there for an interview and was hired on the spot. I now had a new job in a new city.

It wasn't long after our move to Kansas City that my sister called to say that Mom wasn't getting better. On the contrary, she was going downhill. The Crohn's disease had spread throughout her small and large intestines, and the doctors were going to have to remove everything. She would need to undergo radiation treatments, and possibly chemotherapy, as well, just to extend her life by another year at best. She decided to keep herself intact rather than be carved up, radiated, and attached to a tube just to live a little longer.

Several hours into the first day of faculty in-service at the start of the school year, I received a call from the hospital. My mother was dying, and if I wanted to see her again, I needed to come as soon as possible. I was excused from school to head back to Rochester.

What I saw when I entered my mother's room was a very different Mary Kay DuPré from the one I had seen a few months prior. Her face was gaunt, her skin was clammy, and her complexion was as white as could be. I held back my tears and went right over to give her a hug. Her arms felt very weak, yet they surrounded me with strength that seemed to increase as we embraced. We both knew the reason I was there—to say good-bye.

I pulled a chair up to her bed, and she asked how things were going in Kansas City. We talked for a while, and then she dozed off. When she awakened, she was suddenly very energetic. It was as if she knew our time was short and wanted to make the most of it.

We talked some more, and then she raised her hand to my mouth and, with her index finger, touched the mustache that had been above my lip for twenty years. She looked at me and said, "I always loved your face. Could I see it one more time without the hair?" Before those words even fell to the floor, I was on my feet. I went into the bathroom, found the ugly hospital-issue plastic razor, soaped up my mustache, and shaved it off.

I walked back out to the room and sat down again at Mom's bedside. She raised her hand once more and stroked my lip. "There, that's the lovely face I remember. That's my baby." I started to cry, and she patted my face. "It's okay, Chris. I love Him, and I'll see Him soon."

Through my tears, I said, "I know, Mom. I'm just gonna miss you."

A nurse came in to check a reading on the monitor, and the moment passed. Mom and I talked some more until she grew tired again, and then I left for the day.

When I came back the next day, Mom was sitting up in bed with a look that said, "Hey, let's talk." She acknowledged that we'd been through a lot as a family years before, but she wasn't sure how much I really knew about it all, since I was so young at the time. I assured her that I knew a lot less than she did, and that anything she could tell me about my childhood years would be of great value to me.

So, during the next three days, in between checkups and visits, Mom poured out her heart to me, sharing things I'd never heard before. She talked of her marriage to my dad and the breakdown that happened over the years. She talked about the multiple separations that they had gone through, and how it was a "miracle" that I was ever born, let alone conceived.

As she reminisced, she led me through each year of my life, helping me put the scattered pieces I remembered into place. I wish I could have recorded it all; but, knowing my mother, she never would have agreed to that, unless I'd be content with a watered-down version.

By the end of our time together, we had bonded in a way we never had before. Mom was passing me a baton of knowledge that I was now to carry. I realized that she had shouldered an enormous burden over the years, and it had taken its toll. Now, having told so much to me, she looked lighter. I knew she was ready to go to Jesus.

After my final full day with my mother, I headed back to my brother's house. The two of us talked about my time with Mom, and I realized that in spite of all the pain my mother had gone through, she was clean in her heart toward my dad. It made me aware of another dimension of forgiveness I needed to address. I knew I had forgiven my dad for what he had done to me, but I now found myself needing to forgive him again for what he had done to my mother.

That was a big revelation for me. Forgiving my father for what he had done to me was a good first step. But in order for that forgiveness to be complete, I would also need to forgive him for hurting those I loved most. That realization turned on a light for me. From that point on, I would need to make sure that forgiveness was ongoing—not just toward my dad but toward every person in my life: past, present, and future. God has always been very intentional in His forgiveness; I needed to be the same.

The next morning, when I was scheduled to fly back to Kansas City, I headed over to the hospital to say a quick good-bye before heading to the airport. As the moment of my departure approached, I sat on the edge of Mom's bed and just held her hand.

She looked at me and smiled as a tear trickled down one of her cheeks. Then she lifted her hand and once again touched my lip. "My baby boy," she said, over and over. Finally, after we hugged a big, long hug, she held me at arm's length. "Now, you have a wonderful trip home," she said.

My eyes filled with tears as I looked at her and said, "You too, Mom. Have a wonderful trip home."

I got up, blew her a kiss, and began to walk out of the room. I held in most of my tears until I was halfway down the hall, and then the dam burst. With no regard to the people all around, I wept like a baby, walking and weeping right out of the hospital. I walked down the street to my brother's house and waited outside until the flow of tears had ended.

The following week, on the first day of school, I received a call that my mother had just died. I instantly saw her in the presence of Jesus and felt both loss and joy. I would never see her again in this life, but I knew she was finally without pain. I went back to the classroom and finished the day with the knowledge that Mom was seeing the One she loved the most, face-to-face. She was finally experiencing the look of wild love.

12

WILD LOVE

It's been years since my father passed away, but not a day goes by that I don't remember his look of affection toward me. That look, and his gift of wild love, are forever burned upon my heart. You see, that's what it's all about: really seeing the heart that's behind the eyes. My father spent many years as an angry, lonely man, and yet he is remembered by most as a man filled with life and love.

It's not how we start the race; it's how we finish it. My father finished well. That's what's so wonderful about our gracious Father. His mercies are new every morning (see Lamentations 3:22–23), so we can let go of yesterday and begin all over again tomorrow. He throws our sins into a sea of forgetfulness and chooses to remember them no longer. We, on the other hand, usually have a hard time letting go of our sins and weaknesses. Our tendency is to hold tightly to what God has already forgotten. We are often our own worst enemies.

Forgiveness is just the beginning. Yes, we all need to cultivate a life of forgiveness—forgiveness of ourselves as well as others. But once we've tasted God's grace and forgiveness, we need to move on to the heart behind that grace and really get to know the Person behind that forgiveness. We constantly receive His countless gifts of grace, but we become trapped in the cycle of knowing *about* Him instead of really *knowing* Him. It's like reading book after book about a very famous person: we may become experts in the minutiae concerning him or her, but we've never looked into their eyes and seen what's truly inside.

I sometimes want to remove the tag "Christian" from people so they can forget about being part of a group and remember that all God ever wanted to do with man was walk with him in the garden. He didn't desire denominations or factions; He has always been after two things: convincing the human heart that He is good and proving to us, His children, that He is crazy about us.

I hope you're not offended by my use of the word *crazy*. I mean it in its purest sense. One of the less formal definitions of *crazy* is being over-the-top in love, and experiencing extreme passion as a result. What could be more extreme than to leave the glories of heaven to become a man, suffer the worst form of death imaginable, die, and be buried, all because You are in love with someone? That someone is me, and that someone is you.

That's what makes God's love for us a wild love. It's a love that is unrestrained by human hands. No man controls, has ever controlled, or ever will control whom God loves or how deeply He loves. If we, as Christians, believe that our religious practices have some sort of "control valve" on how God thinks or feels about us, and that incorrect actions will incur God's wrath, we are deceived. If I am ever a part of something that makes people question God's love for them, I am doing the enemy's work—not God's.

I'm not dismissing the importance of having people in our lives who can speak the truth to the deepest level of our hearts when we need direction and counsel. Rather, I'm referring to church structures that were built to bring needed order but soon became pillars of oppressive custom wielding more power over our lives than the tender voice of the One who gave His life for us.

Jesus said that we weren't made for the Sabbath but that the Sabbath was made for us. (See Mark 2:27.) In like manner, we weren't made for the church; the church (that is, the idea of a people who gather together, with all their inherent flaws and weaknesses) was made for us. We were not made to meet the needs of the church. We were made for Him. We were made for love.

What is your identity? Are you a Christian? Ok, that's a great start; but "Christian" is not the primary identity God chose for you. It's a label that was created by mankind to identify those who believe in God. That's not a bad thing, but calling ourselves Christians doesn't automatically make us to be lovers of God.

Proverbs 23:7 says, "As [a man] *thinks in his heart, so is he.*" What we believe, specifically, about the nature of God determines how we think. And how we think determines what we do. As believers, do we have within us an identity that will carry us through life? If not, we become slaves to—or, worse, victims of—every emotion and all circumstances that surround us. That is not our destiny.

Years ago, the Lord whispered to me, "Who are you?" When God asks you a question, He's not asking because *He* doesn't know the answer; He's asking because *you* don't know. So, I did not answer Him right away. Instead, I went to the One who knows best. I said to Him, "Okay, Lord, who am I?" His answer confirmed my journey and set my heart, once and for all, in a secure, immovable place. He simply said this: "You are a loved son."

A loved son. Yes, I'm a loved son! That's it. Everything else makes sense after that. As a loved son, I am secure in my Father's love. That love is not dependent on my goodness or faithfulness; it comes from His goodness and faithfulness alone. I'm not held by the promises I may make to God; I'm upheld by God's promises to me.

Therefore, as a loved son, I can become a more loving husband. As a loved son, I can be a more gracious and patient father. As a loved son, I'm a more faithful friend. As the saying goes, "My roots determine my fruit." Ephesians 3 calls me to be *"rooted and grounded in love"* (verse 17), in order that I may *"comprehend with all the saints what is the width and length and depth and height—to know the love of Christ…"* (verses 18–19).

Did you catch that? We need to know God's love in order to comprehend His love. That means my main objective in life is not to prove my love to Him but to know His love for me. I love because He first loved me. I can love only to the extent that I know I'm loved.

It may appear selfish in print: "I'm gonna put God loving me first on my list." Yet, when it's put into practice as a lifestyle based upon relationship, people experience the fruit of your walk, not the sound of your talk. They experience God's love through you, not the secret life of His love coming to you.

A heart that knows the Father's affection is a heart at rest. No longer is performance the driving force of life. People at rest have nothing to prove. Nothing I can do will affect His affection for me or change His love for me. My love, my obedience, my very life, turns from being my Christian duty and instead becomes what it was meant to be: a response of a heart overflowing with love. Freely received, freely given. There's nothing as pure as love freely given, with no strings attached.

Immediately after I was saved, I was ushered into a community where worship was the top priority. A wonderful atmosphere was present time and time again as we gathered to sing and worship the Lord. It wasn't long, though, before "good teaching" and the importance of "well-crafted services" replaced the simple devotion that had been initially prominent. As this shift was taking place, I wrote a song that expressed the confusion I felt in my heart. The first couple of verses went like this:

Where do I go from here?
I'm just a babe, I need some help now.
You've been this way before.
Where do I go?

Where do I go from here?
You say He speaks, how does one listen?
You've heard His voice I know.
Where do I go?

That became my cry: *Lord, where do I go? Where do I aim the rocket of my heart?*

God came to me, face-to-face, and showed me that I was to pursue His wild love. That was my answer then, and it remains His invitation today. As the years have passed, and I've found

158 Wild Love of God

myself as a father and now as a grandfather, my main mission—
my goal in life—has never changed. Because I'm first loved, I
love. As they say, "It's so simple, even a child can do it."

Over the years, as I've shared the story of my father time and
again, I've found many people who deeply ache for reconciliation with their own earthly father. There were never any words
of love between them and their father, and they see no hope.
For many others, their father passed away years before, and they
realize they'll never be able to experience a restored relationship
with their dad.

So, where do they go from here? They go to the same One
who longs to be face-to-face with them. My journey is not meant
to be duplicated. Our testimonies are never meant to be shared
in order to boast or to set people up to believe that what happened to us will also happen to them. Too many people are disappointed from thinking that way.

Instead, our stories are meant to inspire others to find God
for themselves and to know Him. I'm not here to live out someone else's promises. I'm here to know Him and to hear for myself
what He has in store for me. That takes time and that takes relationship. We can dig deeper and deeper into that relationship,
but only if we're convinced in our hearts that He is for us and
that He actually does like us. Believe it! He is right there, waiting for you to accept His wild love.

When we were living in Rochester, our youngest daughter,
who was around four at the time, came to me one day and asked
if she could talk to me. I told her I'd love to talk, and I lifted her
onto my lap. I asked her about her day, and she told me a few
things. Soon, she started to yawn. A few minutes later, she was
sound asleep. I just looked at her, marveling at her beauty, and I
soon found myself focusing on her little toes. They were so cute,

I just wanted to eat them up. Laura came into the room, and I called her over. I said, "Look at her toes. I love these toes."

Years later, when we were living in Kansas City, I was being challenged in the disciplines of my Christian walk. Specifically, I felt that God was unhappy with my prayer life. I was determined to do better, so I set my alarm early in order to seek Him at daybreak. When the alarm went off the next morning, I pulled myself away from my den of warm blankets and slid to my knees next to the bed. I leaned over onto the mattress and started to pray. About forty-five minutes later, I woke up in a puddle of drool. Not only had I not prayed, but I had fallen asleep, right there in His presence. I was ashamed of myself.

As I knelt there, I heard His unmistakable voice. It was so clear, it was as if someone was speaking out loud right there in the room. He said, "I love your toes. I just love those toes." I didn't have a clue what was going on. I knelt there for another moment, and then it hit me: I had done the same thing with my daughter five years earlier. She had come to me in order to spend time with me, and yet, despite her best intentions, she'd fallen asleep in my presence. And all I could remember was how beautiful I thought she was, and how much I loved her and her cute little toes.

Now, here I was, trying to impress God with my new, diligent prayer life, and I'd fallen asleep. Only, His response was not one of disappointment; it was one of celebrating who I was to Him. While I was "out of it," He was looking at my toes. He was enjoying me. That's what He does.

"But, Chris, you don't know me." I hear that all the time. Here's my response: I don't need to know you; I know Him, and that's enough. I'm not saying you should feel licensed to make bad choices because you believe that His love for you will automatically remove every negative consequence. We reap what we sow. (See Galatians 6:7.) We need to know His Word and His ways, and we need to walk in wisdom. That's part of being in relationship with the God who loves us.

But this I also know: God sees our desire to be with Him. We don't always follow through as we'd like to, but He sees our hearts. He knows how we really do long for Him. Again, I'm not advocating a lazy life in God, but I am advocating an honest evaluation of how He sees us. We're His kids. He loves His kids. You're His kid, and He loves your toes. Even that funny one that turns out to the side. He is in love with you. All of you.

A few years after the incident when I fell asleep while in prayer, I was sitting in my living room playing the guitar and singing a David Ruis song, "We Will Dance on the Streets That Are Golden." I loved that song and used it often while leading worship. My youngest daughter came into the living room, sat down next to me, and started to sing with me. She has a beautiful voice and a natural gift for singing harmony.

I was thoroughly enjoying our time together when she suddenly got up and went to her bedroom. I kept playing the song but was sad that my daughter had left. A few minutes later, she emerged from her room dressed in her "dance whites," an elegant outfit that flowed over her beautiful frame. She'd been dancing since the time she could walk and was wonderfully graceful. She began to dance around the room, and above her head she held a delicate white veil that drifted on the air like a sweet perfume. As she danced, I was caught off guard. My eyes started to tear up. My daughter was dancing unashamed before her father. It doesn't get any better than that.

A few minutes into the song, I realized that although I wanted to join the billions of people dancing "on the streets that are golden," at that moment, all I wanted to do was see one person dance—my daughter. A moment later, I heard His voice again. He gently said, "That's how I feel about you. I love the multitudes, but I also love the one. I love to just be with you."

Tears filled my eyes as I heard His affection for me while watching my daughter worship Him in dance. A few minutes later, when the song was supposed to end, I kept playing and found myself singing something else. Within a few minutes, an entirely new song emerged—a song that, for me, was birthed out of one of the most personal, intimate times I've ever had with God.

That simple song has gone on to be sung by many people who have shared a similar testimony with me—that as they sang, God brought healing to their hearts and helped them strip away a false impression of Him as a harsh, cold Father. They have gone on to feel His embrace and to know that He desires to hold them, so they might spend the rest of their lives dancing in His arms of love.

> Dance with me,
> O Lover of my soul,
> To the Song of all Songs.
> Romance me,
> O Lover of my soul,
> To the Song of all Songs.
> Behold, You have come
> Over the hills
> Upon the mountains
> To me.
> You have run,
> My Beloved,
> You've captured my heart.
> With You I will go
> For You are my love
> You are my fair One.

The winter is past
And the springtime has come.

So, where do we go from here? I think we really have only one choice: we move toward wild love. Not just move toward it; we dive into it with all we have and all we are. We run to Him because He is safe and because He is good. (See, for example, Psalm 136:1.) We stay near Him because He holds the words to eternal life. (See John 6:68.) We press into Him because He is love. (See 1 John 4:8, 16.)

We let Him hold us. If we do, one day, sooner or later, we will take the time to look—really look—into His eyes and see what it is we've always needed, what we've always wanted: eyes that look back at us and tell us without words that we are perfectly and completely loved. And when you've been captured by His wild love, you're captured forever.

13

"I THINK I HAVE MY SON BACK"

The original version of this book was unveiled on Father's Day at Catch the Fire, Toronto. For me, it was a dream come true. Not the "I hope to someday be Paul McCartney's best friend" kind of dream. It was a deep, lingering desire of my heart to share what I had lived through in a way that would bring honor to my father and his memory. He was a perfectly imperfect man who found God's amazing grace, just like the rest of us, and decided to use the time he had left on this earth to learn how to love. And he did!

I have been writing songs ever since my father bought me my first guitar—a cheap, small secondhand instrument to help me pass the time while I recovered from my ankle injury. I've been "passing the time" in that way for almost fifty years now. Thanks, Dad!

I've had many thoughts recently about that gift from my father. When he gave me the guitar, I didn't know how to play. As it turned out, the thing wasn't even tuned right, but I had no book to show me the correct tuning, so I went ahead and used it and soon started writing songs. This went on for months until, to my surprise and great delight, someone gave me a book for beginning guitar players. Lo and behold, I discovered I'd had one string tuned wrong the whole time.

Thank God for that guitar book. What a difference one little string can make! When I finally got that thing tuned right, the songs seemed to fly off those strings. Now, I'm not saying that any of those early songs was very good. There were a couple of songs that made it through the years; but, all in all, most of the early tunes were short on substance and long on mediocrity. Still, they were my babies, and I loved them all. Each one helped me become a more proficient songwriter. Therefore, each one served a purpose.

What a difference it makes when one area of our life finally comes into "tune." For me, it was the area of how I saw my father—lowercase "f"—and my Father. For years, I had been locked in a prison of hatred with seemingly no way out. And then, suddenly, I was free.

I was recently reunited with an old friend from my high-school days, and for some reason, the subject of our fathers came up. I told him how much I'd enjoyed his dad, who'd always seemed to take a sincere interest in me when I was around.

Though I knew his dad could get angry from time to time, he was always very kind to me.

Then my friend said something that totally surprised me. He said, "I used to hate your dad." He said it with real conviction! I was shocked, and I asked him why. He said it was because he knew how angry and mean my dad had been to me, and then, when I began to make a name for myself in high-school sports, specifically in the area of track and field, my dad would come around to the practices with a stopwatch, ostensibly just to let everyone know that I was his son.

I had had the same reaction as my friend did when my dad started showing up at my track meets. But my wise coach, after observing my negative response to my father's presence, pulled me aside and gave me a good talking-to. He tried to get me to see that my dad wasn't there with an arrogant heart to try to impress anyone; he was there with a humble heart to build a bridge between us. Being present at my track meets was my father's way of connecting with me, his son.

I shared that with my friend, and he smiled with complete understanding. He could see it now. My dad hadn't showed up for himself. He hadn't showed up just for me, even. He'd showed up for *us*.

My track coach tuned one of the strings within my heart. That tuning process began a new era in my life, one that would lead me to see my father as more than just a man who hurt me. I began to see him as a person who was walking out the old adage, "Hurt people hurt people."

Since the initial publication of my book, I have been inundated with the testimonies of people who have walked down similar paths. I can't have a meeting without someone ending up in tears over of his or her own journey of being either a victim or an aggressor. Regardless, I always remind the person that it's not too late to bring Jesus into the mix, get His heart and His perspective, and then watch what happens.

A couple of months after my book first came out, I returned to Toronto. Almost immediately, one of the pastors came up to me to tell me what had happened to two different families in the congregation. The father of each family had read the book, and the story was almost the same for both men: they saw themselves as both victims of abuse, from when they were young, and the abusers, within their own families. After reading the book, they both gathered their families together and apologized to each member. One man went so far as to wash the feet of his wife and children, asking for their forgiveness and vowing that he would become a new man.

When the pastor shared this with me, I was not just blessed and encouraged; I was undone. It showed me that the message of restoration, forgiveness, and the changing power of God's love is more than a challenging message; it's *the* eternal message of the ages. God loves so much more than we can imagine. Go ahead—imagine it. He loves more!

One of the hesitations I had in writing this book had to do with my dad's side of the family. I worried how they would react. What would they think? What would they say? Would they be angry that I had exposed my father as an angry man, or would they see him through the lens I had shaped by the end of the book, as a man who helped imprint upon my heart the face of a smiling, loving, "I'm proud of you" father?

I was especially concerned about how my uncle Pete would respond. He was the oldest of my father's brothers, and one thing I knew about those brothers was that they looked out for one another. As I've said before, the four had as their motto, "If one of us has a dollar, each of us has a quarter." I was close to my uncle Pete, and I was nervous that this book might damage our relationship.

Well, it didn't take long for the family reviews to start coming in: "Loved it, Cuz!" "What a great book!" "Thanks for writing this. It helped me with so many things I've thought or felt." A few of my cousins went on to say that they had perceived a lot of anger in my father over the years and had wondered how it might have manifested within our home. So far, not one family member has shared a negative response with me.

But Uncle Pete...how did he feel about it? Well, he was his normal, lovely, honest self. He made small talk about the book at a family reunion and let me know that I hadn't dishonored my dad, and that he loved me and respected how I had handled the situation. My heart could finally relax.

As I've shared, a number of years after my parents' divorce, my dad married a wonderful woman named Marian. She was a widow with five children who instantly became my stepbrothers and stepsisters. I had known them growing up, and I liked them all. When my father remarried, I was hoping that he'd mellowed a little and would not repeat his previous role as the abusive father.

It turned out that the younger ones who still lived at home did get an angry man now and then; but, fortunately, as far as I know, they didn't suffer any physical abuse at his hand. They did say that he could be a bit scary now and then, and that they were very aware of where he was and what he was demanding. They also said that as time went by, he mellowed out, so that his bursts of anger were farther apart and not as tumultuous or intense. I believe it was a combination of natural growth and maturity, along with his new steps into a life with Christ. Private though that life was, his faith was nevertheless real and sincere.

One of my stepbrothers contacted me after reading the book. I had never received any prior communication from him, so I was a little nervous to know his reaction. Would he think I'd represented my father in a false light? Had I given out some incorrect information that would come back to haunt me? I was hesitant; but, at the same time, I couldn't wait to read what he had to say. Unlike my cousins, my stepbrothers and stepsisters actually lived with my dad, and so they had their own experiences and stories from sharing a roof with him.

Here's what I read when I opened up the note from my stepbrother:

> Hey, little brother. I just read your wonderful book. Well-done and on target. We should talk. For reasons I didn't understand then, Dave and I were very close, especially during his beginnings of "discovery and healing." At the time, in the mid- to late-1970s, I was on the board of the Mental Health Association and setting up the original EAP (Employee Assistance Program) for the sheriff's office. I noticed telltale behaviors in Dave soon after he became my father. We were solid, but it became apparent that my "hero" had some very serious issues. Our relationship cooled a bit when Mom asked me for a "family intervention," mainly over finances and the relationships with my younger siblings. Unlike your experiences, Dave came to terms with me and opened up. I loved him and always will.
>
> I will shock you with some things; and, yes, in answer to your question in the book…I knew of you, our dad, and the garden. Our Father works in mysterious ways. Your book needed to be written before you and I ever spoke of the past. He, and your dad, now wants me to pull back the curtain. I never thought this time would

come, and I hope it will bring you great comfort, like a kiss on the cheek.

Love ya, little brother.

Bob

Needless to say, I was overjoyed that Bob thought my book was wonderful, as well as on target. His opinion was very important to me, and I couldn't wait to hear what else he had to say. The eldest of five, Bob had been a captain in the Monroe County Sheriff's Department and was now a well-known and respected business owner in the city of Rochester.

We agreed to meet on my next visit to his hometown at his favorite restaurant. I remember driving there, wondering what he could possibly have to say. The summer day was hot, and it was a sweet relief to step into the air-conditioned interior of the restaurant. Bob and I embraced, then found a table. The establishment wasn't very busy, and Bob remarked that he was glad, as that would make it easier for us to have a more honest conversation.

Now I really wondered what was coming.

Once we'd ordered our food, Bob started right in, sharing his thoughts. I could tell early on that he had been carrying these thoughts for a long time. He began by addressing my time with Dad in the garden. I had been under the impression that no one had seen our interaction; at least, no one had ever mentioned it to me.

But Bob shocked me when he said that he had seen the whole thing. When I asked him what he'd seen, specifically, the description he gave matched mine from chapter 9 almost word for word. He told me he'd been sitting in a back room overlooking the family gathering when he saw me approach my father. From his vantage point, it appeared to be a normal greeting between us—a polite handshake, followed by my dad gesturing toward his garden, wanting to show it off to the next person who stepped up, which happened to be me. Bob said that something in my dad's demeanor seemed to change, and that he looked down, when I stopped my dad and said something. Bob thought I might have offended my dad or delivered some bad news. If you remember from chapter 9, I had just told my dad that I wanted to say something about the period of time when he had lived with us.

Bob said that the next move really shocked him. He saw my dad standing there, straight and still as a statue; and then, after a minute or so, I put my arm around him, and my dad began to weep. Bob confessed that he pressed his face against the window to watch what would happen next. When my dad suddenly started bending over, Bob wondered if something was physically wrong with him; but, because I didn't call for help, he thought otherwise and began to understand what was really happening. We were processing our pain, and Bob had a front-row seat.

Then, as you'll remember, it was my turn to get emotional. As my dad began to slowly crumble to the ground, he reached out and grabbed ahold of my waist with his left hand. When he did that, I began to weep and bend over, as well. There we were, in all our glory, bending over and bobbing up and down—even though I believed nobody was watching.

When my dad and I finished crying, we gathered ourselves together and, after a few words, smiles, and laughs, separated. At this point, Bob said, he was awestruck. He knew our history, at least as much as he'd managed to pick up over the years. He was, and is, a wise man who doesn't miss much.

After my dad and I separated after our garden encounter, I went to my wife and asked if she'd witnessed the scene. She had not. I asked a few others, and their response was the same. None of them had seen a thing.

Ah, but Bob had. My dad then walked briskly by the crowd, apparently intent on making his way to the bathroom so he could dry his eyes and present himself as having it all together, but he didn't make it. Bob intercepted him. My dad walked in the house, and when he saw Bob sitting by the back window, he stopped. Bob looked at him a moment, then asked him what had just happened with me in the garden. He said my dad could hardly speak, for he was still overcome with tears; but he finally managed to get out just seven words: "I think I have my son back."

When Bob told me that, I began to cry. It really had happened. It wasn't my imagination, nor did I exaggerate the significance of the event. It happened just as I remembered it. And, most important, something had happened in my father's heart. He had been brought to tears at the thought that he and I could finally have a relationship. It wasn't too late.

Bob went on to share about some of the struggles that my father had had over the years. He continued to have trouble managing his finances responsibly, and he was still prone to angry reactions. But he had sought counseling and was making great attempts to, as Bob said, "become a better man."

As my stepbrother talked, I could feel myself shifting back and forth between pain and laughter, sorrow and joy. Seeing the interaction with my father through his eyes brought home to me the gift of those few minutes spent alone at the garden with my dad. With no one interrupting us, it was an unbroken moment of eternal beauty. It was one of the few unbroken things that had ever happened between us.

As Bob and I continued to talk over lunch, he shared a few more eye-opening facts that I will hold in my heart alone. As I said, my father was a perfectly imperfect man. I learned even more about his imperfections, and yet Bob was able to see the gold that lay within. When we'd finished dessert, and Bob was "all talked out," we spoke of our mutual love and respect for each other and of our gratitude to Dad for what he had brought to our lives.

Bob expressed thankfulness for a faithful, loving husband for his mother, as well as a father to his younger brother and sisters. And my own heart filled with thankfulness as I watched my dad grow in love during our final few years together. I'm grateful for the deep, lasting impression he made on me as he lavished his love upon me on his way to surgery.

As we walked out of the restaurant, I joked to Bob that after our lunch, I now had one more chapter to write. We both laughed, but it turned out to be true. I really did have one more chapter to write. You're reading it.

"*I think I have my son back.*" That statement has played over and over in my mind ever since the day Bob shared it with me. Perhaps it keeps coming back to me because of the number of people who have approached me or written to tell me how much my book meant to them, and then asked this question: "If my father is dead, how can I have the same kind of healing that you had with your father?"

It's not about being physically present with one's earthly father; it's more about one's understanding, as a son or daughter. I was on a journey that didn't end with my dad. It was amazing, and I am forever grateful; but the final destination was never just being comfortable as the son of David DuPré. It was about seeing and understanding God's signs along life's path that were there to lead me into seeing His face, enjoying His smile, and knowing the passion of His heart for me. If humanity is our destination, we will be left without the most important thing... Him!

God desires to have His sons and daughters back. His heart rejoices when He sees us trust Him with our families, our finances, and our dreams. Romans 8:15 says, *"For you did not receive the spirit of bondage again to fear, but you received the Spirit of adoption by whom we cry out, 'Abba, Father.'"* We have been adopted! We're no longer alone in this world. Our Father wants us to come to Him—not just as our Father but as our "Abba Father." That is, our "Papa Father." He wants to be our Papa. When He becomes that, we become more like the sons and daughters we were called to be.

I was recently asked to share my story at a church service, after which I was approached by a man who shared with me that he had been adopted. In my message, I had mentioned that during Bible times, it was not just Jewish custom but Jewish law that a natural-born child could, for whatever reason, lose his inheritance. I had explained this fact in the course of my message because I wanted to drive home the reality that God has adopted us into His family, and we can be assured that He will never separate Himself from us or deprive us of our promised inheritance.

This man wanted to encourage me by saying that not only was I correct about adoption during Paul's time; he himself had been told the same thing when he was adopted as a young boy. It wasn't just ancient Jewish law; it was good old modern-day American law. Adoption equals inheritance! When I was a newly saved believer, I felt bad that I was "only" adopted into the kingdom. Today, now that I understand the full implications, adopted is the only way I want it to be. God chose me to be His son because He wanted to be my Father. He wants you, too! He chose you! He will never leave you, nor will He ever revoke the inheritance He has promised you. *Adopted.* I like it!

One thing I have observed over the years is that the message of God's love is usually appreciated but not always sought after. This trend has been reinforced to me in a number of ways, including how people would rather pay to listen to the next great prophetic word, whether at a conference, in a book, or on TV, than to learn how deeply they're loved so that they might love others well in turn. Don't get me wrong—I love the prophetic. But, to my knowledge, God's personality and nature are not defined as prophetic; they're defined as love. He *moves* prophetically, but He *is* love.

Today, the Christian media seems to prioritize making people aware of what's in it for them. "Read my book, and you'll discover the key to success," or "Attend this conference, and your life will never be the same." My favorite is, "Come and hear what God has in store for you next!"

I'm not knocking the legitimacy of lives changed due to watching a televangelist or attending a conference; I'm simply saying that, for me, change has always come about because of a face-to-face confrontation with the Person of Jesus, not because I discovered the latest view of eschatology, prophecy, or church growth.

I've attended thousands of church services and hundreds of conferences. I love gathering with other people to worship God and to develop a better understanding of who He is, what His Word says, what His mind is thinking, and how His heart feels. Those things are important. But the message of love is often seen as a "lesser truth," often because it's assumed to be something we already know enough about.

Sorry, but I don't believe it's possible to ever know enough about the love of God. I've come across too many people—many of them church leaders—who are drowning in fear, anxiety, and pain, while God's precious love is there waiting for them to see, to understand, and to find refuge in. I once heard someone say he was upset that the pastor had spent all four Sundays of a certain month preaching on the subject of love. "I got it," he said, with no small amount of frustration in his tone.

I don't think he did.

I pray that we will "get it." This book was written with one great purpose in mind: That the readers would, through the story of one man, see enough of God's heart of love to have something within them change forever. I'm not asking too much, am I? All I want is for people to read about an imperfect man who had an imperfect son—two men who, together, through their parallel journeys, found a God who loves more than they could ever imagine, and, in so doing, found each other again…even for the first time.

I pray that through this simple book, every reader will see God's smile more clearly, hear His voice more audibly as He sings His song over His children, and heed His call to come and experience the greatest power in the universe—His extravagant, wild love.

ABOUT THE AUTHOR

Chris DuPré carries within his heart one great desire, that people would know the depths of God's great love for them. He shares the knowledge of one who has seen God's face and knows God's heart. Originally from Upstate NY, Chris moved to Kansas City to work alongside Mike Bickle in establishing the International House of Prayer. Chris recently served as Associate Pastor at Grace Center Church in Franklin, TN, and now is an associate pastor of Life Center in Harrisburg, PA. A pastor, teacher, worship leader, traveling speaker, and spiritual father to many, Chris may best be known for his song, "Dance With Me." He has produced seven albums and published two books, including *The Lost Art of Pure Worship* with James Goll. Parents of three daughters and grandparents of five grandchildren, Chris and his wife, Laura, reside in Harrisburg, PA.